Smart Money Concept 3.0 PRO

Luis Risueño Gómez

Market Manipulations

DEDICATION

With love, I dedicate this book to my beloved sons, Luis and Guillermo Risueño Da Silva. Thank you for giving me your unconditional love, patience, and support throughout the process of writing this book.

Index

1 Introduction

Welcome to the book Smart Money Concept, Pro

What is Smart Money?

The concept of Smart Money encompasses major financial institutions and institutional investors who possess a distinctive ability to foresee market trends even before they are reflected on the charts. In other words: they manipulate the markets. These entities (which include large investment funds, banks and other large institutions) exert a notable influence on the direction of prices, making them a valuable source of information for traders.

What will you find in this book?

In this book, we will not only explore the theoretical foundations of Smart Money, but we will also provide you with:

- **Practical tools and strategies**to operate in an informed and profitable manner.
- **Practical exercises**with 15' and 1' charts, with a 1 to 15 ratio (and the flexibility to explore a 1 to 30 ratio).
- **Interpretation of candle patterns**and the use of specific Smart Money indicators.
- **Psychological and ethical aspects of trading**to help you make responsible decisions.

- **Risk management and operations planning**based on the Smart Money Concept (SMC).

Who is this book aimed at?

- Experts looking to perfect their skills.
- Beginners who wish to understand the market from the inside.
- Anyone who wants to improve their trading results.

What awaits you here?

Through examples and case studies, you will learn about advanced Smart Money Concept strategies used successfully by professional traders which will give you a competitive advantage in the market.

The ultimate goal of this book is to provide you with a solid foundation to trade with confidence and make informed decisions in the financial markets.

Get ready to immerse yourself in the fascinating world of Smart Money Concept and discover strategies that will take your trading to the next level!

2 Smart Money Concept

The concept of Smart Money (or SMC for its acronym in English) refers to institutional investors or "big players" who have access to significant financial resources, privileged information and extensive experience in the markets. These investors are usually: hedge funds, investment banks, asset managers and other large financial players.

The main characteristic of Smart Money is the ability to move large sums of money in the market and take strategic positions based on an exhaustive analysis of financial, fundamental and technical data. Due to their experience and resources, Smart Money often has a competitive advantage over retail investors in terms of access to information and the ability to influence asset prices.

Smart Money is also associated with the ability to: detect emerging trends, identify investment opportunities and anticipate changes in the market, before they become evident to other financial participants. Therefore, many retail investors pay attention to the behavior of Smart Money and interpret its movements as a signal to guide their own investment decisions.

In short, the concept of Smart Money encompasses a set of large financial actors who make use of various advantages in relation to others of lesser weight to carry out strategic operations from which to obtain profits. For example, institutional investors (such as hedge funds, investment banks and pension funds, as we mentioned above), have access to advanced resources and analysis that allow lucrative investment opportunities to be identified before they reach the general public. These, by having a deeper understanding of the markets, have the ability to carry out significant operations and influence the price of assets through their actions.

Thus, retail investors are usually guided by the behavior of Smart Money when making investment decisions. Observing how these big players act can provide clues or arguments regarding future market trends and directions, allowing retail investors to better position themselves when trading. In short, Smart Money expresses the influence and power of large investors over the markets through movements based on information and privileged analysis; That said, it is a tool to take into account for small investors and their operations.

3 The fundamentals of financial success

In this chapter, we will develop how to set clear financial goals and build a solid financial plan based on smart money management, according to the SMC criteria. These fundamentals will not only define the direction of our finances, but will also provide a framework for making informed and strategic decisions that bring us closer to our financial aspirations.

The first step towards financial success is the definition of goals, because they act as a compass that guides every decision we make: from our daily purchases to long-term investments. Therefore, if we set objectives framed in a SMART approach (that is, specific, measurable, achievable, relevant and limited in time), our goals will not only guide us in a strategic and coherent way, but they will also become goals. tangible and concrete things that we can reach with determination.

It must be recognized that financial goals are not static: they evolve as our personal, professional and economic circumstances and perspectives change. Therefore, their ability to review and adapt must ensure that our financial plan remains relevant and effective over time.

So, creating a solid financial plan is the next step in our journey to success. This plan consists of daily money management and long-term planning to ensure financial stability at each stage of life. First, thoroughly assess our current situation, and then strategically align goals and available resources.

A realistic budget is essential in this process, since it allows us to control our income and expenses effectively while adapting to our needs and objectives. Flexibility and a regular review of the financial plan will allow us to anticipate obstacles and adjust our strategies as necessary.

In short, a comprehensive perspective that establishes objective financial goals and develops a solid financial plan is the foundation of intelligent money management which provides us with direction, structure and empowerment to make informed and strategic decisions, paving the way to a solid financial future. , satisfactory and possible.

4 Smart Money Deep Analysis

If this chapter had a subtitle, it would undoubtedly be "The power of knowledge and strategy in financial success." Here we will explore how Smart Money, with its strategic approach to financial management, goes beyond simply managing large amounts of capital. In addition, we will delve into how institutional investors and large financial entities, with their deep knowledge and experience, have the ability to influence the market and anticipate movements with precision.

Through specialized equipment, access to certain information and technical analysis, Smart Money has the ability to identify prosperous investment opportunities. This represents a crucial competitive advantage over the rest of the market through information prior to being public. At the same time, the entities that comprise it not only adapt to the market, but also influence it due to their powerful volume of capital, participation in monetary policy and the ability to anticipate and set trends. Thus, it generates significant movements in prices that are closely followed by smaller players.

Investors and traders closely follow Smart Money stocks, using their movements as an invaluable guide to make informed decisions and anticipate potential changes. These sophisticated strategies include the use of derivatives, hedging and arbitrage techniques, allowing them to maximize profits in a complex and constantly changing market.

Understanding how these entities operate is crucial for investors looking to successfully navigate the complex world of investing. Beyond simply observing the large amounts of money at stake, it is crucial to understand all the knowledge, experience and strategies behind Smart Money as they provide a privileged view when making financial decisions; These must be supported by solid information, arguments and strategies, in order to contribute to the achievement of our goals contemplated in our financial plan.

5 Volume and liquidity analysis

Within this section, we will see the key tools to understand the behavior of Smart Money, such as volume and liquidity in financial analysis, important concepts to understand the actions of the SMC.

On the one hand we have the volume, which represents the amount of financial assets that are bought and sold in a given period. This is a key indicator of activity and interest in a given asset. On the other hand, liquidity refers to the ease with which an asset can be bought or sold without affecting its price. Both notions are crucial to understanding how Smart Money operates in the market.

The joint analysis of volume and liquidity makes it possible to identify the participation of Smart Money in the market, anticipating its movements and making decisions according to the situation. For example, a significant increase in the volume of a company's shares may indicate purchases by Smart Money, anticipating a rise in price. This is a signal that many could interpret to operate in relation to the objectives that each one has.

In addition, analysis allows us to: detect accumulation and distribution patterns, confirm existing trends, and detect divergences between price and volume, which can signal possible changes in market direction. Interpretation of these changes in volume and liquidity is also crucial. A sudden increase in volume may be indicative of Smart Money involvement, and therefore a possible significant movement in price. Also, volume during trends can confirm trend direction, while the relationship between volume and price can offer clues about Smart Money's intentions.

Likewise, the comparison of volume and liquidity between different assets can provide substantial information, identifying the assets in which greater interest and therefore greater activity is observed.

In summary, the analysis of both volume and liquidity are necessary and appropriate tools to understand the different behaviors of Smart Money in the financial market. This allows us, as investors, to make the pertinent decisions to anticipate possible changes in it, always in an informed and reasoned manner, without neglecting our planning of the stated objectives.

6 Price manipulation by Smart Money

In this chapter we will explore the strategies used by Smart Money to influence market prices, as well as historical examples of manipulation and its consequent impact on retail traders.

Financial institutions employ various techniques to manipulate prices, including volume, news, orders, closing prices, and options. Although these practices are considered illegal in many countries and can result in sanctions, the objective of influencing prices in this way means obtaining great economic benefits.

Some historical examples of this kind of manipulation that we can consider here are: the "Flash Crash" of 2010; "the Libor scandal" of 2012; the "Pump and Dump" scheme in cryptocurrencies (artificial price inflation through misleading statements); and "frontrunning" operations (the operator takes his own purchase or sale position and generates profits by sensing what his client's actions will cause). All of these events have had a significant impact on smaller players, resulting in large losses and above all affecting confidence in the financial markets.

Therefore, it is crucial that retail traders are informed about these types of practices and take the necessary measures to protect themselves: research and analyze before investing; diversify investments; pay attention to market news and events; Use risk management strategies and seek professional advice if necessary.

In other words: price manipulation by Smart Money is a reality. Given this, retail operators must be alert and take appropriate precautions to protect their investments and minimize risks.

7 Forex Basics

The foreign exchange market, better known as Forex or Foreign Exchange, is the largest and most liquid financial market on the planet. Within this market, we find a wide variety of participants: from banks and financial institutions to multinational companies, governments, investors and retail traders. Currencies from around the world are constantly exchanged here, resulting in a dynamic environment full of trading opportunities.

These transactions are carried out in currency pairs. That is, evaluating the value of one currency in relation to another, such as the EUR/USD pair representing the relationship between the euro and the US dollar.

Forex trading operates 24 hours a day, five days a week. Even though it does not have a centralized physical location; since transactions are carried out electronically through a global network of banks and institutions. Given these characteristics, it is clear that this currency market is driven by a series of factors which include not only economic aspects such as interest rates, inflation and employment; but also by geopolitical events such as elections, wars and policies of different central banks.

The constant fluctuation of exchange rates due to their uniqueness is fertile ground of opportunities for traders, but also of possible risks. That is why it is essential to properly manage these risks to protect one's capital and maximize rewards.

For this reason, in the next chapter we will display a series of fundamentals for traders. Knowledge and understanding of these are of utmost importance, since they provide a set of key tools for decision making, such as: interpreting price movements; manage risks associated with operations; identify trends; Perform fundamental analysis and seize opportunities

Let's review: the foreign exchange market is a complex and dynamic world, subject to economic or external risks. Even so, education and knowledge are essential and are key to the success of our financial plan. Therefore, the following chapters will provide the relevant tools and knowledge necessary to navigate this exciting world with confidence, skill and the necessary skills.

8 Different types of charts used in technical analysis

In price action analysis, charts play a vital role in providing visual information about the movement and development of prices in the market. There are several types of graphs in this type of analysis, each with its own characteristics and benefits depending on the desired approach. Below, we will list some of the best known:

Line charts: They are the simplest and most basic. They represent the direct connection between the closing prices of an asset in a specific time period. These closing prices are linked by a straight line, allowing general trends and patterns in price movements to be identified.

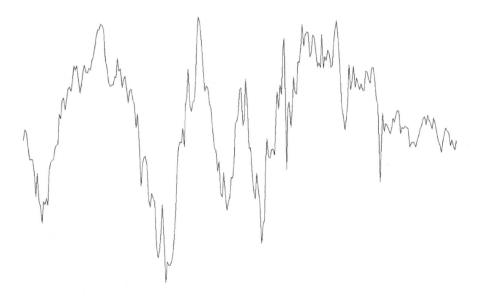

Bar Charts- Show the open, close, high and low price information in the form of vertical bars. Each of these bars represents a specific time period and thus provides a more detailed view of the price action. Their upper part represents the maximum price that has been reached, while their lower part represents the minimum price. The horizontal line on the left side of the bar indicates its opening price, while on the right side a horizontal line represents its closing price.

14

Japanese candlestick charts: widely used in price action analysis. Each of these represents a specific time period and displays information about the open, close, high and low prices. Its central part, known as the "body", exposes the difference between the opening price and the closing price. If the body is filled or colored, this indicates that the closing price is lower than the opening price. On the contrary, if the body is empty or uncolored, it means that the closing price is higher than the opening price. Its thin lines, called "wicks" or "shadows," which extend from the body, represent the maximum and minimum prices reached during said period.

Point and figure graphs: Unlike the previous charts, these are based on significant price movements and not time. They use point and figure formations (hence the name) to represent changes in price direction. These types of charts are mainly used to identify reversal patterns and long-term trends.

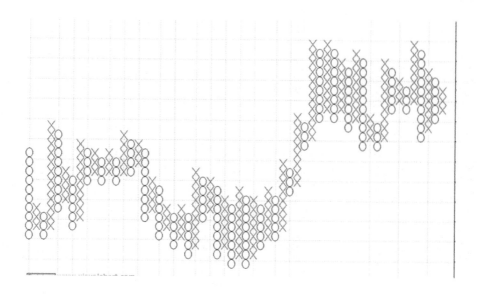

Each type of chart has its own advantages and disadvantages. Therefore, traders should choose the one that best suits their style, preferences, and goals. It should be noted that it is always important to understand how to read and interpret each of these graphs when making decisions (both operations and the selection of graphs). In this way, traders will be able to act in a consistent, informed and solid manner during technical analysis.

9 Analysis of market structure

9.1 How to identify the areas of accumulation and distribution of Smart Money

In this chapter, we will delve into the analysis of the market structure and how to identify the areas of accumulation and distribution of Smart Money. Below is a suggested route for this topic:

9.1.1 Significant Supports and Resistances

Support and resistance levels are key areas in technical analysis that can indicate the accumulation and distribution of Smart Money. This often seeks to accumulate large positions in support areas where prices have shown a strong rebound in the past. Likewise, it seeks to distribute its positions in resistance areas, where prices have shown difficulty in breaking upwards. Watching these levels when they are significant on the charts can provide clues to Smart Money areas of interest.

These measurements are essential for technical analysis, as they offer critical insight into possible price declines in the future. For example, on a market chart during a downtrend, support acts as a "floor." When an asset falls to that level, buyers will step in, preventing the price from falling further and causing a rebound. That support zone can manifest itself in different time frames and is considered a solid base for the market.

On the other hand, resistance represents a "barrier" on the chart that is difficult for the price to overcome during its uptrend. When the price reaches this level, the sellers take control, thus causing a decrease in the price. Similar to support, resistance can be seen as the "ceiling" of the market.

Both levels are crucial for traders, as they allow them to plan their movements. Identifying a support or resistance level that has been forced repeatedly without breaking can be a signal to open a long or short position, respectively. These phenomena can even help determine the exit points of a trade, which will maximize profits or minimize losses.

It is important to remember that these levels are not foolproof, and therefore can be broken. When this happens, the market is likely to head towards the next support or resistance level depending on the case. Furthermore, this breakout can also be used as a trading opportunity, opening new positions in the direction of the recent price movement.

It should be added that not all support and resistance levels are the same: lower levels can temporarily slow a trend, while higher levels have the potential to stop and even reverse a trend completely. In turn, repeating tests at a level increases their validity, further strengthening their importance in the market and in the mentality of traders.

Finally, it is worth noting that support levels can become resistance and vice versa, depending on market phenomena. This behavior can offer clues about future price movements and be useful in developing effective trading strategies.

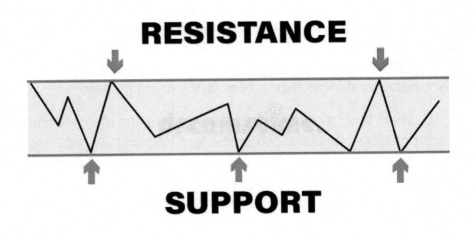

Support and Resistance

9.1.2 Consolidation patterns

Smart Money often accumulates positions during periods of market consolidation. These patterns can be identified as narrow price ranges or sideways channels. During these consolidation phases, Smart Money accumulates or distributes assets discreetly without causing significant price movements. Identifying such patterns can help identify areas where positions are being taken.

The rectangle pattern occurs when the price of an asset moves within a horizontal price range for an extended period of time. Here, the price orbits between two lines of support and resistance, forming what appears to be a rectangle on the chart (hence the name).

The support line represents the price level at which the asset is expected to bounce upwards, while the resistance line indicates the price level at which the asset is expected to fall. As the price moves within the range, the buyers and sellers balance each other and the rectangle pattern consolidates.

When the price finally breaks through the resistance line or the support line, a trading signal is produced: if the price breaks the resistance line, this indicates that the buyers have surpassed the sellers, and therefore, it is expected that the price rises; On the contrary, if the price breaks the support line, the sellers have surpassed the buyers, and the price is expected to decline.

Traders can use this pattern to identify possible entry and exit points in the market. A common strategy is to wait for the price to break through the support or resistance line and then enter a trade in line with the direction of the breakout. It is important to note here that the rectangle pattern, like any other type, is not always an accurate signal. Therefore, traders should also use other indicators and analysis to confirm the trading signals they are interpreting.

9.1.3 Order flow analysis

This analysis in relation to price action tracking can provide valuable information not only about the presence of Smart Money, but also the areas of its accumulation and distribution. For example, if a large number of buy orders are observed as prices rise, this may reveal a buildup of the aforementioned. Another applicable example is if you see a large number of sell orders as prices fall, as it may indicate a distribution. Analyzing order flow in combination with price action can provide a clearer picture of Smart Money's areas of interest.

9.1.4 *Volume analysis*

Volume is another important aspect when identifying the areas of accumulation and distribution of Smart Money. Due to accumulation, it is possible to see an increase in volume as assets are purchased. Otherwise, during the distribution there may be an increase in volume as assets are sold. Paying attention to changes in volume taking into account the relationship with price movements helps identify areas where Smart Money is operating.

9.1.5 *Use of technical indicators*

Technical indicators are useful when identifying areas of accumulation and distribution of Smart Money. Namely, the accumulation/distribution indicator helps determine whether there is greater accumulation or distribution of assets in a given period of time. Other indicators, such as the money flow index or the volume oscillator, can also provide signals about the presence of Smart Money and its shares in the market.

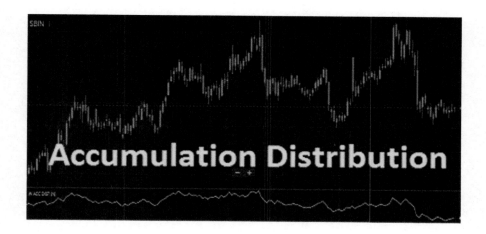

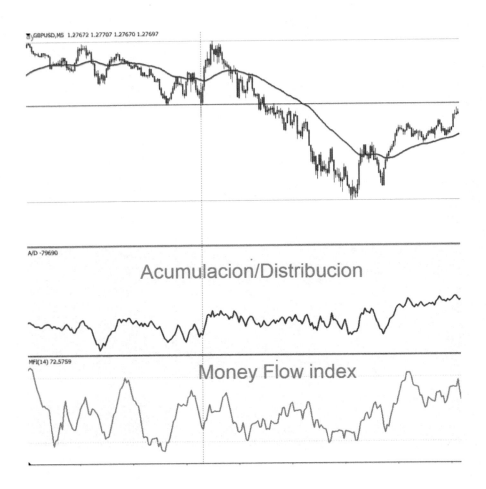

GBPUSD,M5 1.27672 1.27707 1.27670 1.27697

A/D -79690

Acumulacion/Distribucion

MFI(14) 72,5759

Money Flow index

It is important to remember that identifying areas of Smart Money accumulation and distribution requires careful analysis as well as a combination of different tools and approaches. There is no "magic formula" to accurately identify Smart Money actions; But by applying these aforementioned analysis methods, traders can increase their understanding of the market and make more accurate decisions based on different perspectives and indicators.

In other words, by analyzing the market structure it is possible to identify areas of accumulation and distribution using different tools such as: analysis of supports and resistances, consolidation patterns, order flow, volume and the use of technical indicators. By combining them, traders can gain a better understanding of Smart Money actions and use that information to make more informed decisions on the market and its context-specific phenomena.

9.2 Using patterns and technical analysis to understand market structure

In this section, we will explore how to use patterns and technical analysis to interpret market structure and gain insight into Smart Money stocks. Below is a suggested development for this topic:

Reversal patterns, as well as head and shoulders, double top, double bottom and triple top patterns (which we will discuss later), provide possible clues regarding market structure and the possible accumulation or distribution of Smart Money. These patterns form after an established trend and can indicate a possible reversal in market direction. Observing the formation of these patterns allows us to identify areas where Smart Money may be making strategic decisions.

9.2.1 *double roof*

A double top is a bearish reversal pattern that occurs when the price of an asset reaches a resistance level twice in a relatively short period of time and then experiences a downward reversal. Its name derives from the formation which resembles two consecutive peaks on the chart, with a valley in the middle.

This pattern, also known as "the 'M' formation," usually appears at the end of an uptrend, indicating a possible change in direction toward a downtrend. In this formation, its consecutive peaks or maximums are characterized by reaching the same price level. Next, we will describe the processes of formation of a double top.

During an uptrend, prices make higher and higher highs and lows. However, in this pattern, the last high fails to surpass the previous one, but instead stops at a level similar to the previous one (first top). This mid-range rise suggests a weakness in the upward trend, which is a first warning sign.

At first, the trading volume increases during the uptrend; But when the first top is formed, the price rise is accompanied by high volume, while the subsequent correction is carried out with lower volume. At the second top, the price rise occurs with low volume, indicating a lack of conviction in the uptrend.

Once the second top is formed, prices begin to fall towards a support level defined by the base of the tops, possibly breaking the uptrend line. This drop may be accompanied by low trading volume. Furthermore, prices may not cross the downward bullish trend line immediately, and may rise again and thus overcome the resistance formed by the double top.

If prices manage to break down the base level of the double top, the chart formation is completed, indicating a change in the bearish trend and thus providing a sell signal. Although an increase in volume at this point could increase signal reliability, it is not an essential requirement.

The final confirmation of this trend change occurs by observing how prices behave once the breakout occurs. If prices try to rise again, but find resistance at the broken support line and then fall again, they confirm the trend change. At this point, a downtrend line can be drawn joining the second top and this second lower high.

After the double top formation is completed, it is possible that prices will fall to at least the level defined by the height of the pattern, which is projected downward from the base. The breadth and duration of the formation can influence its impact, with these formations (wide and long-lasting) being more significant. Finally, to validate this pattern, it is recommended that the two highs be separated by at least one month in their duration.

Similar patterns are those of triple tops, which follow a similar analysis, although with three or more consecutive maximums, being also important the monitoring and evolution of trends, supports and resistances in conjunction with graphic and technical analysis. The separation between the highs in this case does not need to be as wide as in the case of double tops.

If we look at the charts, we identify that the first peak

represents a failed attempt by the price to overcome the resistance, followed by a fall. Afterwards, the price rises again and reaches the same resistance level, forming the second peak. If the price fails to break through its resistance level for the second time and starts falling again, the double top pattern is confirmed.

Many traders often consider the double top to be a bearish signal, so they look to sell the asset when the price breaks its support level (the valley between both peaks). In some cases, the price may fall by the same amount as the distance between the resistance and support level, which would provide a profit target for the trade.

Double Top Pattern

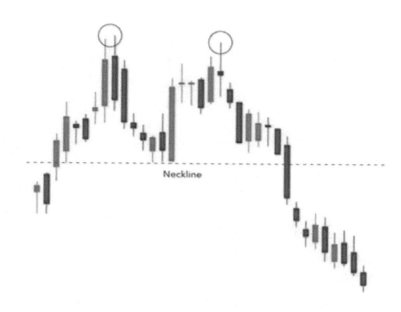

Representa el final de una tendencia alcista y el inicio de una bajista

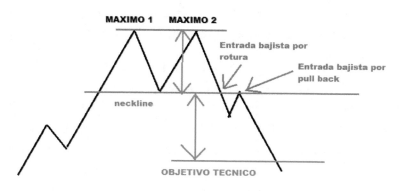

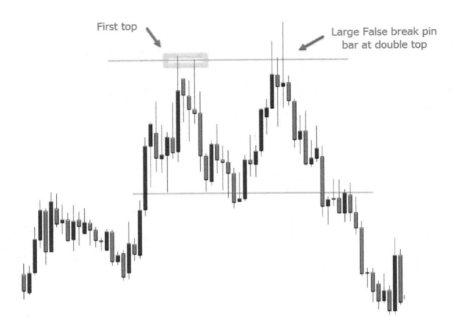

First top

Large False break pin
bar at double top

9.2.2 *Double floor*

Before we dive into identifying the double bottom, it is important to understand chartism and chart analysis, as this type of pattern is a chart figure used in this type of analysis. Chartism refers to the branch of technical analysis that studies price charts to look for patterns that help predict the future price of an asset. This approach is based on the belief that past patterns can be repeated in the future.

The double bottom is one of the figures observed in this type of analysis, and is especially popular among practitioners of "day trading" (operations within the same trading day). It is a bullish reversal pattern formed after a downtrend. It is made up of two equal or very similar relative lows in the price of an asset, separated by a peak between them. This peak represents a resistance level that must be overcome to confirm the formation of the pattern.

After the first low is formed, the price usually bounces and falls back towards the level of the last low. If the price fails to break through this level and begins to rise again, the second minimum occurs. Confirmation of the pattern occurs when the price breaks upwards the line connecting the two peaks.

The double bottom is an indication that the previous downtrend may be coming to an end and that a new uptrend could be underway. Traders often interpret this phenomenon as a buy signal, with a stop loss located below the support level formed by the pattern's lows. However, it is important to note that this is not always a reliable reversal signal and it is always advisable to use other technical analysis tools to confirm any intuition or readings before making trading decisions.

This trading pattern is an investment strategy that takes advantage of the identification of a price which remains in a limited range for a certain time. This leads to buying an asset when the price approaches one of the extremes of the range. Such a strategy is especially useful in markets with low volatility, where prices appear stuck between two levels.

If you've ever felt like trading is like riding a roller coaster, experiencing wild swings from stability to chaos in a matter of seconds, then you're familiar with the concept of a double bottom. This term is used to describe the tendency to return to previous levels after a sudden change.

To correctly identify a double bottom, traders must observe price action and pay attention to other indicators such as volume and moving averages. Pattern confirmation occurs when price breaks higher after the second touch of the support level, indicating a potential change in trend direction.

In other words, the double bottom is a valuable tool in a trader's arsenal; as it provides information on possible entry and exit points in the market. Understanding how to identify and use this pattern can greatly improve your ability to take advantage of and profit from profitable trading opportunities.

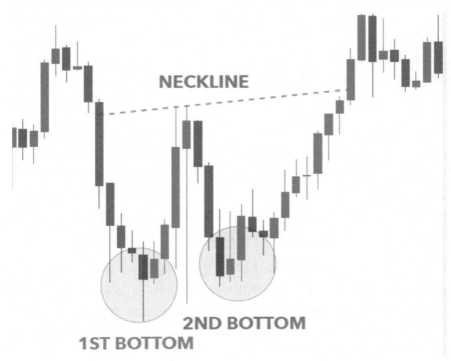

NECKLINE

2ND BOTTOM

1ST BOTTOM

Doble suelo

Double floor

9.2.3 Shoulder head shoulder and inverted

The Shoulder-Head-Shoulder (HCH) pattern is a technical analysis figure used to forecast possible changes in the

35

trend of an asset. This is made up of three consecutive peaks of which the middle peak (the "head") is higher than the other two, (the "shoulders"), the latter being lower and symmetrical to each other.

At the time an HCH is formed, prices are in an uptrend and then begin to decline forming the first shoulder. Then prices rise again, forming the head. Finally, prices fall again finishing the second shoulder, thus completing the pattern. When the neckline is broken, i.e. the line connecting the lowest points of both shoulders, the uptrend is expected to reverse to a downtrend.

On the other hand, the Head-Shoulder Inverted (HCHI) pattern, although similar to the HCH, here the figure is made in a bearish trend: prices reach a minimum, then rise to form the head and finally return to lower to form the shoulders. When the neck line is broken upwards, the downtrend is expected to reverse to an uptrend.

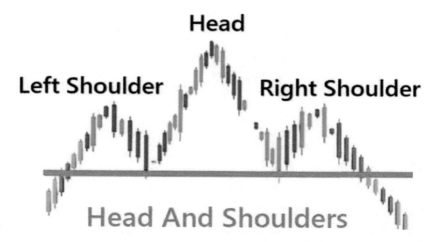

Hombro cabeza hombro invertido   H   H

C

NECKLINE

LEFT SHOULDER

RIGHT SHOULDER

HEAD

Continuation patterns These patterns, such as flags, triangles and wedges, can indicate market consolidation and the accumulation or distribution of Smart Money. They form within an existing trend and suggest that the trend is likely to continue once the pattern completes. Identifying these types of patterns can help traders identify areas of Smart Money interest and thus take advantage of their trading opportunities.

Bandera Inversa

REVERSE FLAG

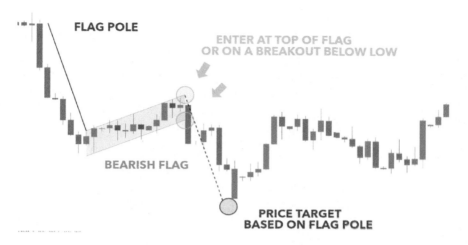

9.3 The triangle pattern

Within technical analysis, the triangle pattern is a type of trend continuation pattern that forms when price moves in one direction and then consolidates into a triangular pattern before continuing in the direction of the original trend. There are three main types of triangles in this type of pattern: the ascending triangle, the descending triangle, and the symmetrical triangle.

Firstly, the ascending triangle is formed when the price moves up and forms a horizontal resistance line. At the same time, it generates a series of higher lows that form an ascending trend line. Both lines converge at a future point, thus creating a triangle. Technical traders can look for a break above the horizontal resistance line as a sign that the uptrend will continue.

On the other hand, the descending triangle happens when

41

the price moves down and forms a horizontal support line. At the same time, a series of lower highs form a descending trend line. These lines converge at a point in the future, making the triangle concrete. Traders can track a break below the horizontal support line as a sign that the downtrend will continue.

Lastly, the symmetrical triangle is formed when the price moves up and down in a broader consolidation pattern, forming two converging trend lines. Unlike the aforementioned, in this case there is no clear horizontal line of support or resistance. Technical traders can look for a break above the downtrend line or below the uptrend line as a signal of a possible continuation of the trend respectively.

Generally, triangle patterns are a useful tool for technical traders as they provide an early indication of a possible trend continuation. However, a breakout does not always occur after the formation of a triangle, so it is important to wait for some confirmation before making trading decisions.

In our system we will not take the triangle pattern into account, but we will explain it for didactic purposes to know it and be able to delve deeper in the future.

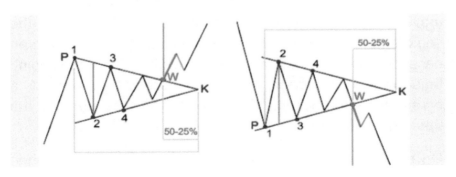

Trend analysis: Identifying bullish, bearish or sideways trends can provide signals regarding the accumulation and distribution of Smart Money. During an uptrend, you may be accumulating positions as prices rise. Conversely, in a downtrend, you may be allocating positions as prices fall. Therefore, trend analysis can help traders align their strategies with the general direction of Smart Money.

Use of technical indicators: both the relative strength index (RSI), the MACD (Moving Average Convergence/Divergence) or the moving averages contribute to the identification of overbought and oversold conditions, divergences and signs of trend change. Combining pattern analysis with the use of technical indicators provides a more complete view of the market structure and Smart Money actions, as well as a comprehensive perspective to plan our movements.

Volume analysis: Observing changes in volume can provide clues to accumulation and distribution processes; since an increase in this during a price movement could indicate an active participation of Smart Money. Furthermore, volume analysis in relation to price patterns and technical indicators can operate as a further confirmation of our market structure hypothesis.

With everything listed, the use of patterns and technical analysis are very valuable instruments not only to understand the structure of the market but also to obtain information about Smart Money actions. In addition, the identification of reversal and continuation patterns, trend analysis, the use of technical indicators and volume analysis are key concepts for developing market strategies. By combining these tools and techniques, traders can increase their potential by identifying areas of Smart Money interest and thus make the most of trading opportunities that arise from different situations.

10 Accumulation and distribution patterns

10.1 Description of specific patterns used by Smart Money

In this tenth chapter, we will explore specific accumulation and distribution patterns used by Smart Money in the market. These patterns can provide clues to the stock's actions and help traders identify possible entry and exit areas. Below is a series of some of these patterns along with their respective descriptions:

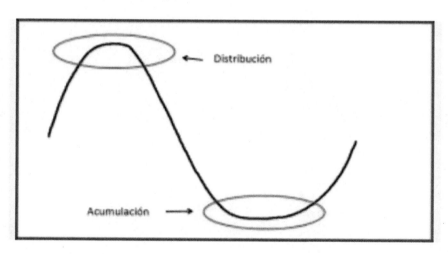

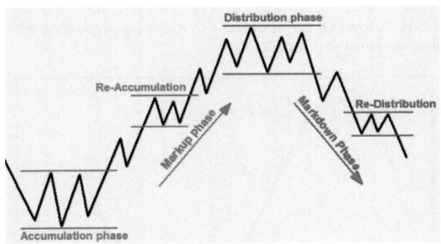

10.1.1 Spring

A spring is an accumulation pattern that occurs after a drop in price. During this phase, Smart Money buys assets at low prices, which creates a "trap" for panic-selling traders. Spring is characterized by a rapid rebound in price after hitting a new low, resulting in accumulation by Smart Money.

10.1.2 Shakeout

The shakeout is a distribution pattern that occurs after a rise in price. During this phase, Smart Money sells assets at high prices, creating a "trap" for traders who overbuy. The shakeout is characterized by a rapid drop in price after reaching a new high, indicating a distribution by Smart Money.

Shakeout

10.1.3 Upthrust

The upthrust is a distribution pattern that occurs when price briefly breaks above a key resistance level and then quickly falls back below it. This indicates that Smart Money has been selling assets as prices reach resistance levels, creating a false bullish signal.

10.1.4 Absorption

Absorption is an accumulation pattern in which Smart Money gradually accumulates assets while absorbing (hence the name) sell orders from retail traders. During this phase, the price may remain in a tight range or even show a slight upward trend. The absorption indicates that Smart Money is accumulating positions without causing large price movements.

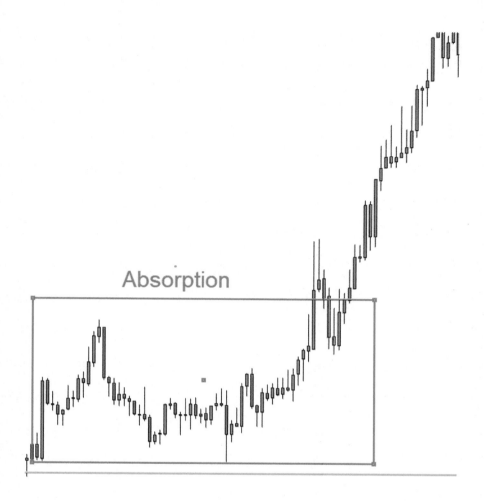

10.1.5 Supply/demand test

The supply/demand test is a pattern that occurs after an accumulation or distribution phase. During this phase, the price moves back towards the previous accumulation or

51

distribution zone and a test of supply or demand occurs. If the price cannot break below the accumulation zone or above the distribution zone, it may indicate that the Smart Money has absorbed the supply or demand and is ready to push the price in the desired direction.

Distribution

Offer/Demanada test

It is important to note that these aforementioned patterns do not guarantee specific movements in the market, and therefore should be considered within the broader context of technical and fundamental analysis. Additionally, it is advisable to use other tools and confirmations to support the identification of such patterns.

In summary, the accumulation and distribution patterns used by Smart Money, such as those we have just seen (spring, shakeout, upthrust, absorption and supply/demand test), can provide valuable clues and indications about the actions of Smart Money in the market.

10.2 How to recognize patterns on price charts

Recognizing accumulation and distribution patterns used by Smart Money on price charts requires careful observation and the use of appropriate technical analysis tools. The following pages will detail some of these tips to recognize these patterns:

Identify trend changes- Accumulation and distribution patterns often occur at key trend reversal points. We must pay attention to areas where the price stops following an established trend and begins to consolidate or reverse.

Observe the volume- This is a key indicator to identify accumulation and distribution patterns. During accumulation, volume tends to be low in the initial phases and then increase as Smart Money purchases assets at low prices. During distribution, volume tends to be high in the initial phases and then decrease as Smart Money sells assets at high prices.

Analyze the pricing structure: It is necessary to observe the formation of price patterns that indicate accumulation or distribution, narrow ranges, consolidations and reversal or continuation patterns. These patterns are usually visible on price charts and can provide signals about Smart Money stocks.

Use technical indicators– These can help confirm accumulation and distribution patterns on price charts. For example, the Relative Strength Index (RSI) and cumulative volume can provide additional signals of divergences or changes in the Smart Money share.

10.2.1 RSI (Relative Strength Index)

The relative strength index (RSI) is a technical indicator used in technical analysis to evaluate the strength of a trend and detect possible changes in it. It is calculated through a mathematical formula that compares the magnitude of recent gains with recent losses in a given period of time. One of the uses of the RSI can be to identify divergences, which can provide entry and exit signals for trades.

To use the RSI when identifying divergences, we must first understand what a divergence is. Generally speaking, a divergence occurs when the price of an asset moves in one direction and the indicator moves in the opposite direction.

Therefore, a bullish divergence occurs when the asset's price is decreasing while the RSI is increasing; and in the opposite direction, a bearish divergence occurs when the price of the asset is increasing while the RSI decreases.

To find such divergences, traders must compare price movements with the RSI. If the price is making lower highs and the RSI is at higher highs, we can reason that a bullish divergence is occurring. On the other hand, if the price is making higher lows and the RSI is making lower lows, a bearish divergence is taking place.

These divergences can be a sign that price momentum is changing and can be used to enter a trade in the opposite direction of the current price momentum. For example, if a bullish divergence is identified in a bear market, it could be a sign that the price is about to reverse its trend and rise. In this case, a trader could enter a long position in the asset.

However, it is important to remember that the RSI is not an infallible tool, so divergences do not always result in a trend change. Thus, it is advisable to use other instruments to confirm the hypotheses made using RSI.

Regarding how to rate an asset using the RSI, we can start with the fact that this indicator varies between 0 and 100. A value above 70 is considered to indicate that an asset is overbought, while a value below 30 indicates that an asset is oversold. Traders often use the RSI to determine whether an asset is overbought or oversold, which can help them make buy or sell decisions.

The moment the RSI line approaches 100 indicates that the

asset is in a strong uptrend; while, if it is close to 0, it indicates a strong bearish trend. If the RSI remains above 50, it means that the trend is bullish, while below 50, the trend is conceived as bearish.

It is necessary to keep in mind that the RSI, as with other indicators developed earlier in this book, is not perfect and can sometimes provide false signals. Therefore, it is important to use other indicators and technical analysis tools to reinforce the RSI clues to make well-formed and consistent trading decisions.

The RSIwe will use it with its standard configuration, which is 14 periods.

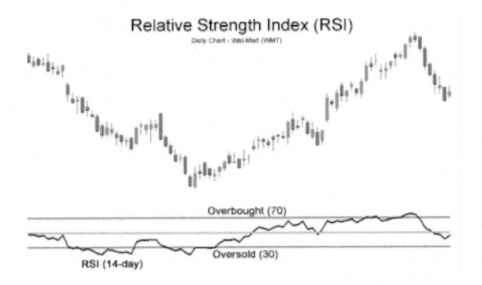

Relative Strength Index (RSI)

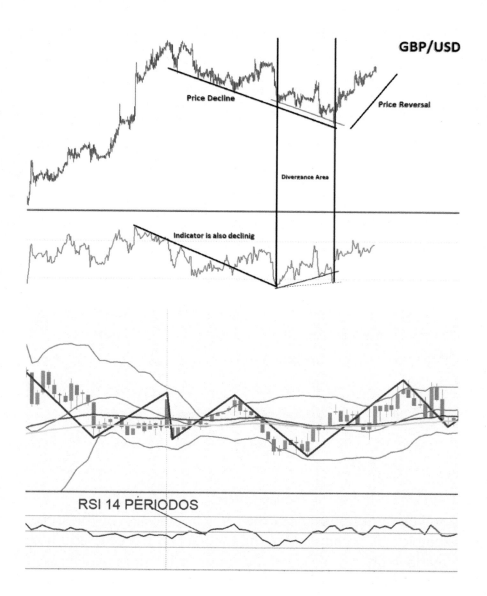

DIVERGENCIA CON EL RSI

Analyze previous patterns: The analysis of historical examples of accumulation and distribution patterns and how they developed in the past allows us to become familiar with the characteristics and signs that usually accompany these phenomena.

You always have to remember that pattern recognition on price charts is subjective and requires practice and experience. It is extremely important to note that not all accumulation and distribution patterns will be accurate on all occasions, so it is always advisable to use different instruments when analyzing and in this way build a complete and organic perspective of the different indicators, depending of the general market context at a given time.

With that said, to recognize accumulation and distribution patterns used by Smart Money in price charts, it is essential to observe: trend changes, analyze volume, study the price structure, use technical indicators and learn from previous patterns. By combining these techniques, traders can improve their abilities to identify and take advantage of opportunities associated with the accumulation and distribution of Smart Money.

11   Candlestick and price pattern analysis

11.1 Explanation of candle patterns and how Smart Money uses them to its advantage

In the pages that follow, we will develop candle patterns and how Smart Money uses them to its advantage. Candlestick analysis is a popular mechanism which provides information about the psychology of different market participants. Below we will present some common candle patterns and how Smart Money takes advantage of them:

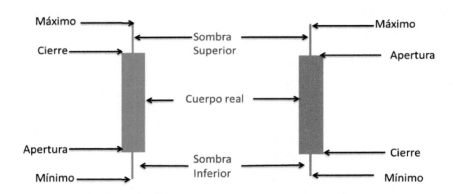

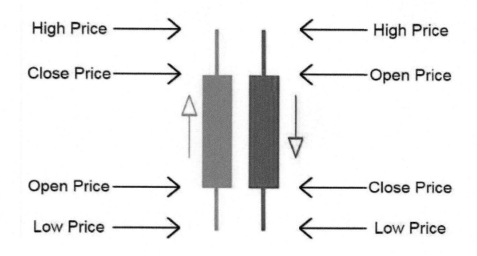

11.1.1 Hammer

The hammer is a bullish candle pattern that has a small lower shadow and a relatively large body. Indicates a possible bullish reversal after a bearish trend. Smart Money can use this pattern to accumulate positions at low prices before an upward move.

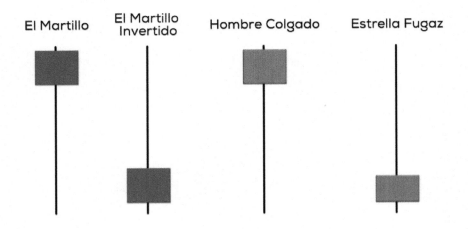

El Martillo | El Martillo Invertido | Hombre Colgado | Estrella Fugaz

HAMMER CANDLESTICK PATTERN

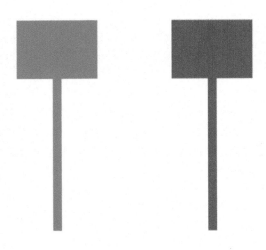

11.1.2 Shooting Star

The shooting star is a bearish candle pattern that has a small upper shadow and a relatively large body. Indicates a possible bearish reversal after an uptrend. Smart Money can use this pattern to distribute positions at high prices before a downward move.

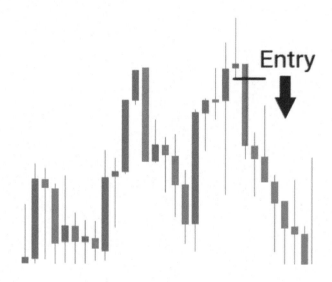

11.1.3 Doji Patterns

The Doji pattern is a candle that has the same opening and closing price, resulting in a very small body. It may indicate indecision in the market. Smart Money can use Doji patterns to assess lack of direction and prepare for possible accumulation or distribution.

Dragonfly Doji

11.1.4 Engulfing

The Engulfing pattern occurs when a candle completely engulfs the range of the previous candle. A bullish Engulfing can indicate a possible upward trend change, while a bearish Engulfing can indicate a downward trend change. Smart Money can use these patterns to anticipate and participate in significant market movements.

Bullish Engulfing Pattern

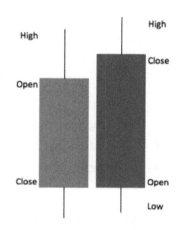

Bearish Engulfing Pattern

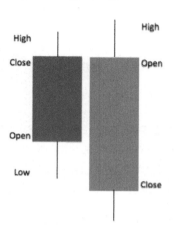

Smart Money uses these candle patterns as another tool in its repertoire to make decisions. In addition to identifying candle patterns, you also pay attention to their location in relation to important support and resistance zones, Fibonacci levels, or other technical indicators relevant to your objectives.

Importantly, candle pattern analysis should be combined with other technical analysis tools and consider the overall market context. Not all candlestick patterns are accurate on all occasions, and it is essential to perform a thorough analysis before making trading decisions.

In summary, Smart Money uses candle patterns such as the hammer, shooting star, Doji patterns, Engulfing and others to identify possible trend changes and trading opportunities. These patterns provide signals about market psychology that we can take advantage of in relation to our goals.

11.2 How to interpret and apply patterns in trading

Interpreting and applying candlestick patterns in trading requires understanding their meaning and how they relate to the market context. Here are some steps to interpret and apply these patterns effectively:

Recognize the pattern: Let's pay attention to the shape, body size and shadows of the candle. Let's make sure we understand what specific pattern we are looking at, whether it is a hammer, a shooting star, a Doji, or any other pattern.

Evaluate the context- Observe the current market trend, support and resistance levels, and any other relevant signals or indicators. This will help us determine if the candle pattern has greater meaning and validity in that specific context.

Confirm the signal: Do not depend on a single candle pattern to make trading decisions. Seeking additional confirmation through the use of other tools and technical analysis is always necessary. For example, tracking confirmation of a bullish candlestick pattern via an increase in volume, a rising moving average crossover, or other technical indicators that support the signal.

Establish an entry and exit strategy: Once the candle pattern has been correctly interpreted and the signal has been confirmed, we must establish an entry and exit strategy. Define entry points, stop-loss and take-profit levels according to the information provided by the candle pattern. We must also consider factors such as risk management and risk/reward ratio.

Monitor and adjust- Once the trade is made, it is important to monitor market development and make adjustments if necessary. We have to observe how the price behaves after the formation of the candle pattern and make adjustments to your stop-loss and take-profit levels if the situation requires it.

Let us remember that no candle pattern guarantees success on all occasions. It is essential to combine candle pattern analysis with other technical and fundamental analysis tools and techniques to obtain a more complete view of the market.

Thus, we have seen that to interpret and apply candlestick patterns in trading, we must: recognize the pattern, evaluate the context, confirm the signal, establish an entry and exit strategy, and monitor and adjust as necessary. Using these patterns as an additional tool in your technical analysis arsenal in combination with what we have read above will lead us to make increasingly professional and experienced decisions.

12 Areas of high probability of operation

12.1 Identification of areas in which Smart Money usually carries out significant operations

Throughout this chapter we will examine the areas in which Smart Money tends to carry out significant operations in the market. Identifying these zones gives traders an advantage when looking for trading opportunities. The following pages present some common areas where Smart Money usually operates:

Key Supports and Resistances– Support and resistance levels are areas where the price has shown a tendency to bounce or reverse in the past. Smart Money tends to operate there due to the high concentration of buy or sell orders that can influence the price.

Fibonacci Levels- These are key levels derived from the Fibonacci sequence used in technical analysis. Smart Money often pays attention to levels such as 38.2%, 50% and 61.8%, to identify possible entry or exit areas.

12.1.1 Fibonacci levels

Fibonacci levels are a series of price levels used in technical analysis to determine possible support and resistance levels on a chart. These levels are based on the Fibonacci number sequence, a mathematical series in which each number is the sum of the two preceding numbers (0, 1, 1, 2, 3, 5, 8, 13, 21, etc.) .

The most commonly used Fibonacci levels are 38.2%, 50%, 61.8%, 78.6%, and 100%. These levels are calculated by measuring the distance between two significant points on the graph; for example, the minimum and maximum of a price movement.

The 38.2% level represents a shallow correction and is considered the first major retracement level. The 50% level is the average level and is often used as a profit-taking target. The 61.8% level is an important level and is considered the strongest retracement level in most cases. If the price moves above this level, it can be expected to continue until the 100% retracement.

Fibonacci levels are also used in combination with other technical indicators to confirm buy or sell signals. For example, if the price of an asset reaches a Fibonacci level and there is also an overbought or oversold signal on the RSI indicator, this can be a sell signal.

It is important to note that although Fibonacci levels can be useful in identifying possible support and resistance levels, they are not always accurate and should not be used as the only tool for making trading decisions.

Market turning points- These are areas on the chart where the market has shown a significant change in price direction. These points are usually followed by an accumulation or distribution by Smart Money before a major move.

Candle patterns: Like reversal candles or continuation patterns already seen in this book, they can indicate areas where Smart Money is taking positions. These patterns form through the interaction between supply and demand and can provide signals about future price direction.

12.1.2 Breakouts

Breakouts occur when the price breaks a key resistance or support level. Smart Money can take advantage of these breakouts to enter or exit positions, as they can indicate a change in market dynamics.

Breakouts

It is important to keep in mind that these high probability trading zones do not guarantee successful results every time. Just as we repeat in other sections, it is necessary to combine the analysis of these areas with other technical and fundamental analysis instruments and techniques to confirm the signals and make informed decisions in relation to our financial plan.

Summarizing the aforementioned: identifying the areas in which Smart Money usually carries out significant operations, such as support and resistance levels, Fibonacci levels, market turning points, candle patterns and breakouts, are of great contribution for traders when tracking trading opportunities, especially with a higher probability of success and more developed skills. By understanding these areas and combining them with the aforementioned tools, traders can improve their ability to trade alongside Smart Money and take advantage of market trends by increasing their profits, depending on their respective goals and objectives.

12.2 How to take advantage of zones to make more informed trading decisions

For traders to make stronger trading decisions, it is necessary to take advantage of areas where Smart Money performs significant operations. Here are some tips for this:

Signal confirmation: both input and output. For example, if a key resistance level is identified in an area where Smart Money typically trades, this could confirm a sell signal generated by a technical indicator.

Risk management: These zones can be useful for establishing stop-loss and take-profit levels. Placing the stop-loss above a resistance or support level can reduce the risk of the price expelling us from the market before a significant movement. Likewise, setting the take-profit in an area where Smart Money usually takes profits can increase the chances of making profits.

Volume analysis- If this is high as the price approaches a trading zone, it may indicate higher participation and confirm the importance of that zone. Increasing volume can be a sign of Smart Money taking action and can provide greater conviction for making trading decisions.

Observing price patterns– For example, if a bullish reversal candle is observed in a support zone, it may indicate a possible bullish reversal.

Track Price Action- If the price bounces or holds, this may indicate a level of participation and validation of the zone. It is important to watch how the price reacts in such areas to get clues about the future direction of the market.

Already mentioned before, but it is useful to emphasize it: no strategy or area is infallible, especially in isolation. It is essential to carry out a thorough analysis and manage potential risks when making decisions.

With this said, here we have reviewed some ways to take advantage of the areas where Smart Money usually performs significant operations, which involve using these areas as confirmation of indications for our movements. These can be: managing risk effectively, analyzing volume, observing price patterns and following price action. By combining them with other analysis tools studied in previous chapters, we have a solid basis to decide with greater and better criteria and thus increase our chances of success.

13   Use of indicators

13.1 Description of specific indicators
designed to track Smart Money activity

We will explore some specific indicators designed to track Smart Money activity in the market. These indicators can provide valuable information about the stocks of large financial institutions and help traders make more informed decisions. Below are some examples of these indicators:

Accumulation/Distribution Line (AD Line): is an indicator that shows the accumulation and distribution of an asset based on volume. It allows you to follow the activity of Smart Money by analyzing whether large investors are buying or selling. If the AD Line shows a constant increase, it indicates accumulation by Smart Money, while a constant decrease indicates distribution.

Volume Weighted Average Price (VWAP): is an indicator that calculates the weighted average of the price based on volume. It helps identify the price levels at which Smart Money has made significant operations. If the price approaches or bounces near the VWAP, it may indicate the presence of Smart Money.

On-Balance Volume (OBV)- Measures the flow of volume in relation to price changes. Helps identify the accumulation or distribution of Smart Money. If the OBV shows a constant increase while the price remains relatively stable, it may indicate accumulation by Smart Money. On the contrary, if the OBV shows a constant decrease as the price rises, it may indicate distribution.

Net Volume- Shows the difference between the purchase volume and the sale volume in a given period. If the Net Volume shows a positive balance, it indicates that there are more buyers (possibly Smart Money) in the market. On the contrary, a negative balance indicates that there are more sellers.

Open Interest: It is an indicator used mainly in the futures and options markets. Shows the total number of open contracts on an underlying asset. An increase in Open Interest may indicate the entry of large institutions or institutional investors into the market.

These are just some examples of indicators used to track

Smart Money activity. It is important to remember that no indicator is infallible and that it is necessary to combine several indicators and analysis tools to obtain a more complete view of the market.

Indicators designed to track Smart Money activity can provide valuable information about the actions of large financial institutions. They can be used in combination with other analysis tools to make more informed trading decisions. It is essential to understand how to correctly interpret and use these indicators to make the most of their potential in the market.

13.2 How to use indicators in making trading decisions

Using Smart Money indicators in making trading decisions requires understanding how to correctly interpret them and combine them with other analyzes and tools. Here are some guidelines to use these indicators effectively:

Signal confirmation: Indicators can provide signals about the activity of large financial institutions. However, it is important to use these indicators in conjunction with other technical and fundamental analyzes to confirm the signals. Look for the convergence of different indicators and signals before making trading decisions.

Trend identification: For example, the AD Line can indicate whether there is accumulation or distribution by Smart Money. Use these indicators to determine the general direction of the market and align your trades accordingly.

Identification of key levels- For example, the VWAP can show the price levels at which the Smart Money has made significant trades. Use these levels as reference points to set entry, stop-loss and take-profit levels in your trades.

Risk management: Don't rely solely on Smart Money indicators to make trading decisions. Use sound risk management and set appropriate stop-loss levels to limit losses in the event of adverse market movements. Also consider the appropriate position size in relation to your capital and risk tolerance.

Continuous monitoring: indicators require constant monitoring. Watch the indicators evolve as the market develops and adjust your trading accordingly. Maintain a flexible and adaptable approach as Smart Money activity and market conditions change.

Let us emphasize again that no indicator is infallible and that it is important to have an overview of the market using different tools and analysis. Also, practice patience and discipline in your trading approach and don't rush into making decisions based solely on Smart Money indicators.

Use Smart Money indicators as an additional tool in your analysis and trading decisions. In the previous pages we have seen a series of tips: confirm signals with other analysis, identify trends and key levels, properly manage risk and continuously monitor indicators to adjust your trades as necessary. Use these indicators as part of a complete trading strategy tailored to your own goals and preferences.

14 Psychology of Smart Money

14.1 Exploring the Smart Money mindset and strategies

Understanding the psychology behind Smart Money can be invaluable for retail traders, as it provides insight into how these large financial institutions make decisions and manage their positions. Below we will present some key aspects of the psychology of Smart Money:

Patience and long-term perspective- Smart Money generally takes a long-term perspective and is not affected by short-term market fluctuations. They have the ability to wait and hold positions for long periods, taking advantage of long-term price movements.

Exhaustive analysis: Smart Money dedicates significant time and resources to conducting thorough analysis before making investment decisions. They use sophisticated mathematical models, fundamental and technical analysis, as well as inside information to evaluate investment opportunities and minimize risks.

Risk management: is aware of the importance of proper risk management. They use techniques such as portfolio diversification, setting stop-loss and using derivative instruments to protect their positions and limit potential losses.

Market manipulation- They use strategies such as accumulation and distribution, creating false movements and inducing panic in retail traders to take advantage of price fluctuations.

Use of insider information: Although the use of inside information is prohibited and illegal, there are cases in which Smart Money can have access to it or use its influence in the markets to obtain advantages. It is important to highlight that insider trading is illegal and is not available to retail traders.

It is essential to understand that retail operators do not have the same level of resources and access to information as Smart Money. However, by taking into account the psychology and strategies used by it, retail traders can adjust their approach and take advantage of some of the tactics and approaches used by large financial institutions.

The Smart Money mentality is characterized by patience, a long-term perspective, thorough analysis, risk management, the ability to manipulate the market and, in some cases, access to insider information. By understanding these aspects of Smart Money psychology, retail traders can adjust their approach. trading and make more informed decisions in the market.

14.2 How to adapt the Smart Money mentality to improve your own operations.

While retail traders do not have the same resources as Smart Money, there are aspects of their mindset and approach that can be adapted to improve our own operations. Here are some ways to do it:

Take a long-term perspective: Don't just focus on short-term market movements, develop a long-term mindset. Recognize that trading success is built through consistent and well-informed decisions over time.

Perform a comprehensive analysis– Spend time and effort conducting thorough analysis before making trading decisions. Use technical and fundamental tools, research and obtain information from reliable sources. The more informed you are, the better prepared you will be to make informed decisions in the market.

Properly manage risk: Prioritizes proper risk management, just like Smart Money does. Set stop-loss limits and define the size of your positions based on your risk tolerance and available capital. Proper risk management will help protect you against significant losses and maintain stability in your trading account.

Learn to recognize and take advantage of opportunities- Watch and learn how Smart Money does it. This means being attentive to patterns of accumulation and distribution, as well as other indications of the activity of large financial institutions. Learn to identify high probability areas and use this information to make more informed decisions in your operations.

Maintain discipline and patience: Both are key to successful trading. Smart Money knows that not all operations are profitable and that long-term results are what matter. Maintain the discipline to follow your trading plan and the patience to wait for the right opportunities before taking action.

It is important to note that adapting the Smart Money mentality does not imply using illegal or unethical practices, such as the use of insider information. Instead, it is about taking positive aspects of your approach and applying them within the legal and ethical limits of trading.

By adapting the Smart Money mindset, you can improve your own trading by taking a long-term perspective, conducting thorough analysis, properly managing risk, taking advantage of opportunities, and maintaining discipline and patience in your trading decisions. Always remember to operate ethically and within the legal limits established in the financial markets.

15 Trading strategies based on Smart Money

15.1 Introducing popular strategies using SMC

Trading strategies based on the concept of Smart Money (SMC) seek to take advantage of the movements and activity of large financial institutions in the market. Below, I present some of these best-known strategies:

Volume Tracking Strategy- is based on trading volume analysis to identify areas where Smart Money is active. A significant increase in volume is sought at key levels, indicating the involvement of financial institutions. Traders can look for entries based on these volume levels and use appropriate risk management techniques to take advantage of potential Smart Money driven moves.

Accumulation or distribution breakout strategy: focuses on identifying accumulation and distribution patterns used by Smart Money to take positions in the market. Traders look for significant breakouts of these patterns, indicating Smart Money's entry in a specific direction. Using technical analysis techniques, traders can track opportunities when a valid breakout occurs, aiming to make profits as the price moves in the expected direction.

Divergence strategy: It is based on identifying divergences between the price movement and an indicator related to the volume or activity of the Smart Money. For example, if the price is reaching new highs while the indicator shows a decrease in volume, it could indicate Smart Money intervention. Traders can use these divergence signals to make decisions, looking for opportunities for trend reversal or continuation.

News and events tracking strategy- Traders can follow relevant news and events to get an idea of how Smart Money, which has access to inside information, can act accordingly. For example: earnings announcements, monetary policy decisions or important economic news can generate significant movements in the market, and you can try to take advantage of these opportunities through appropriate and relevant strategies.

These strategies, although based on observation and analysis of Smart Money activity, do not guarantee unequivocal success. It is always important to carry out proper risk management, use additional analysis techniques and adapt strategies according to your own style and risk tolerance according to your plans. Let us remember that trading carries risks, so it is essential to carry out a complete analysis and use appropriate management techniques to maximize opportunities and minimize losses.

15.2 Examples of practical applications of these strategies.

These detailed examples below offer a practical view of how to apply strategies based on the Smart Money concept in real trading situations:

Volume Tracking Strategy- Seeing a significant increase in volume at a major support level in a Forex currency pair can indicate Smart Money involvement. Entering a long position with a set profit target and an appropriate stop-loss is one way to take advantage of this situation, always considering risk management.

Accumulation or distribution breakout strategy– Identifying a distribution pattern in an asset and seeing a convincing range breakout with a significant increase in volume can signal Smart Money intervention to the downside. Opening a short position after the breakout, with a clear stop-loss and profit target, is one way to capitalize on this opportunity.

Divergence strategy- Recognizing a divergence between the price and volume indicator can indicate a lack of Smart Money participation and a possible reversal of the uptrend. Opening a short position with stop-loss and defined profit target can be a way to take advantage of this situation, always with adequate risk management.

News and events tracking strategy: When important economic data is published, for example employment data, Smart Money can anticipate the results and position itself accordingly. Following the market behavior after these events and taking long or short positions based on the price reaction can be an effective strategy to take advantage of Smart Money stocks.

These examples demonstrate how strategies based on Smart Money can be applied in different trading contexts. However, it is essential to remember that each trade must be carefully evaluated based on specific market factors and your own trading strategy. Practice and experience are essential to make informed and well-founded decisions in the

16 Risk management in trading

16.1 Importance of proper risk management when operating with Smart Money

Throughout this section, we will develop the importance of implementing proper risk management when trading the SMC. While these strategies can offer lucrative opportunities, they also carry inherent risks that must be managed efficiently. Here are some key reasons why proper risk management is crucial in Smart Money trading:

Capital protection- Proper risk management is essential to protect one's capital from potential significant losses. Although Smart Money can provide reliable signals and patterns, there is always a chance that a trade may not go as expected. By setting stop-loss levels and determining appropriate position sizes, you can limit losses and protect your capital from adverse market movements.

emotional preservation- Trading can be emotionally challenging, especially when money is at stake. Proper risk management helps you avoid impulsive or emotion-based decisions by giving you an objective framework to make informed decisions. By having a clear risk management plan and following it with discipline, you can reduce the stress and anxiety associated with trading and maintain mental clarity to make rational decisions.

Taking advantage of opportunities- By determining position size and stop-loss levels appropriately, you can manage your market exposure optimally and be prepared to take advantage of opportunities when they present themselves. Additionally, proper risk management helps you avoid excessive concentration on a single trade, allowing you to diversify and take advantage of a variety of opportunities in the market.

Improved long-term consistency- By establishing clear rules regarding risk management and following them consistently, you can avoid impulsive mistakes and maintain solid discipline in your trading approach. This will help you

86

avoid large losses and maintain balance in your trades over time.

When trading the SMC, it is essential that you establish proper risk management as an integral part of your trading strategy. This involves: determining appropriate position sizes, setting stop-loss levels, setting realistic profit targets, and maintaining consistent discipline in your trading approach.

Remember the element of uncertainty that exists in each operation, and that there is no total guarantee of success in trading. However, by properly managing risk, you can protect your capital, reduce the emotional impact of trading, seize opportunities effectively, and achieve long-term consistency in your results.

16.2 How to protect against losses and maximize profits

In this section, we will explore key strategies and practices to protect against losses and maximize profits when trading SMC. Below are some measures you can consider:

Set stop-loss levels- This is a predetermined level at which you close a trade if the price moves against you. It is a crucial tool to limit losses and protect your capital. By setting stop-loss levels appropriately, considering market volatility and price structure, you can protect yourself against excessive losses. Remember that stop-loss levels should be placed logically, based on technical and fundamental analysis, and should not be emotionally adjusted during the trade.

Use take-profit orders– Like stop-loss levels, take-profit orders allow you to set predetermined levels at which you close a trade and lock in profits. Setting realistic profit targets based on technical and fundamental analysis allows you to maximize your profits and ensure you don't miss out on lucrative opportunities. Upon reaching your profit target, close the trade and take the profits, avoiding the temptation to be too greedy and wait for even bigger profits.

Diversify your operations- Diversification is an important strategy to protect against significant trading losses. Instead of focusing on a single asset or a single type of trade, consider diversifying your trades across different financial instruments, currency pairs, and strategies. This helps spread risk and reduces reliance on a single trade for profit. Remember that diversification should be based on sound analysis and should not involve trading excessively or without a proper understanding of the assets you are trading.

Perform technical and fundamental analysis– This will provide you with valuable information on market movements and possible trends. By combining both approaches, you can get a more complete picture of market conditions and make informed decisions. Technical analysis will help you identify price patterns, key levels, and entry and exit signals, while fundamental analysis will provide information on economic events, news, and factors that could affect prices.

By using both approaches, you can protect yourself against rash trades and increase the likelihood of success.

Follow proper capital management- will protect you against excessive losses and help maximize profits. This involves: determining the appropriate position size in relation to your total capital, establishing exposure limits and avoiding taking excessive risks in a single transaction. A prudent and disciplined approach to capital management will maintain a proper balance and avoid large losses that could negatively affect your trading account.

It is worth remembering that protecting against losses and maximizing profits involves a balanced and disciplined approach to your trading strategy. There are no guarantees in the market and there will always be risks involved. However, by applying appropriate risk management measures, using technical and fundamental analysis, diversifying your trades and following prudent capital management, you can increase your chances of success in Smart Money trading.

17   Smart Money Operation Planning

17.1 How to create a solid trading plan based on SMC

In this section we will take a look at how to create a solid trading plan based on the Smart Money Concept. Having a well-defined plan gives you a consistent structure and a clear roadmap for your operations, which will help you make informed and disciplined decisions. On the following pages there are some key steps for this task:

Define your objectives: Start setting your goals as a trader. What do you want to achieve in the Forex market? What goals do you have? Are they realistic and measurable? Are they long or short term? All of this will provide you with a framework to evaluate your operations and measure your progress.

Establish your risk profile: Evaluate your tolerance and define how much you are willing to risk on each trade. This will help you determine the size of your positions and set acceptable maximum loss limits.

Conduct a market analysis– Use relevant tools that are beneficial to your analysis. Identify the currency pairs or financial instruments that have the greatest potential for movement controlled by Smart Money. It also analyzes price patterns, key levels and relevant economic events that may influence the market.

Identify entry and exit areas: Do it based on market analysis. Use tools such as: candle patterns, trend lines, support and resistance levels, and other technical analysis tools to determine the most favorable entry and exit points.

Set stop-loss and take-profit levels- Determine both levels based on your market analysis. These will allow you to manage risk and protect your profits. Make sure you set these levels logically and consistent with the expected market movement.

Manage your capital- Establish clear rules. Define the size of your positions in relation to your total capital and set appropriate exposure limits. Avoid taking excessive risks in a single operation and diversify your operations in different financial instruments.

Keep track of your operations- Includes entry and exit, stop-loss and take-profit levels, and any relevant observations on your activity. This will help you evaluate your operations and learn from your successes and mistakes.

Review and adjust your plan: Do it periodically, especially when you consider it necessary. Markets are constantly changing, and it is important to adapt your plan to new conditions, tools and learnings.

Although these strategies provide an advantage in making informed decisions in the Forex market, trading success primarily depends on discipline, patience, and the ability to adapt to market conditions. Follow your planning diligently and maintain the right mindset to face the challenges of Smart Money trading, this way you will get closer to your goals consistently and constantly.

17.2 Key Considerations When Planning and Executing Operations

These considerations will help you improve your trading decisions and maximize your chances of success. Below we present some of them:

Exhaustive analysis: Before any operation, carry out an exhaustive analysis of the market using both technical and fundamental analysis. Consider price patterns, prevailing trends, key support and resistance levels, economic events, and any other relevant information that may influence the asset price. The stronger your analysis, the more informed your decision will be when trading.

Risk management: it must be done properly in the world of trading. You should set stop-loss and take-profit levels according to your risk profile and market analysis. Consider your position size in relation to your capital and set appropriate exposure limits. Remember that preserving your capital is essential to maintaining your ability to operate in the long term.

Patience and discipline: the SMC is based on identifying the operations with the highest probability of success; However, this does not mean that all your trades will be profitable. It is important to always have patience and discipline to continue with your trading plan even when you have to face trades that result in losses. Do not get carried away by emotion or impulsivity and maintain discipline in your decisions, only then will you remain on track towards your goals and objectives.

Adaptability- Because financial markets are dynamic and constantly changing, it is crucial to be flexible and adjust your trading plan according to market conditions. If your initial analysis does not go as expected, don't be afraid to adjust your strategies or even exit the trade if necessary. Adaptability allows you to make informed decisions in real time, safeguard your capital, and re-approach objectives with greater experience.

Continuous learning: Always seek to improve your skills and knowledge. Read books, participate in courses, attend seminars and stay up to date with the latest trends and developments in the financial markets. Learn from your past trades, both winning and losing, and use that experience to improve your future decisions. This will allow you to build a plan of higher quality and adaptability thanks to previous knowledge and experiences.

emotional control: Don't let fear or greed influence your decisions. Remain objective and calm, even in situations of high volatility, as those moments are what will test your emotions. The ability to make rational, analysis-based decisions is crucial to long-term success, so we should not neglect our organization and discipline just for passing emotional moments.

Once again it should be noted that trading involves risks and there is no guarantee of results. However, by considering everything described above, you will have a wide range of tools when planning and executing your operations based on the SMC. In addition to being better equipped for eventual decision-making, you will be able to maintain your profile and stability over time without falling into emotions or moments that could alter our planning. Thus, you will be able to not only maintain, but constantly get closer and closer to your goals and objectives.

18   Success case study

18.1 Analysis of real cases in which operators have used SMC

Throughout this chapter we will examine a series of real cases in which operators have successfully applied the Smart Money Concept. Studying this style of cases will provide you with practical examples of how SMC principles and strategies can generate positive results. Having made this presentation, some notable examples:

Case 1: John, an experienced trader, used volume and liquidity analysis to identify Smart Money activity in the forex market. He noted a significant increase in volume at a key support level, indicating accumulation by large institutions. He took a long position based on this signal and managed to make significant profits as the price recovered.

Case 2: María, an intraday trader, specialized in identifying Smart Money distribution areas. She used technical analysis to identify reversal patterns on price charts and combined this information with volume analysis to confirm Smart Money activity. She took advantage of these distribution areas to take short positions and made consistent profits by capitalizing on price declines.

Case 3: Carlos, a long-term trader, used the identification of high trading probability zones based on the Smart Money Concept. He conducted a thorough analysis of the market and identified areas where Smart Money used to enter and exit significantly. He used these zones as entry points for his long-term trades and managed to earn consistent returns as the price moved in his favor.

These success stories that we have just presented highlight the importance of understanding and applying SMC within trading. We see that successful traders use tools such as: volume and liquidity analysis, identification of areas of accumulation and distribution, price patterns and other specific indicators to make informed and profitable decisions.

However, it is worth noting that each operator will have their own approach and will adapt the Smart Money Concept to their personal style and preferences. We can even intuit from previous cases that each one adapted depending not only on the situation but also on his own perspective and aspirations. Whatever the case of success, the common factor in them is the understanding and intelligent application of the principles and strategies of SMC.

To highlight: by studying these success stories, you will be able to obtain valuable ideas and knowledge to improve your own operations and increase your chances of success in the financial market. Remember that trading involves risks, and it is essential to combine knowledge of the Smart Money Concept with proper risk management and a disciplined mindset to achieve consistent long-term results, as we saw in the examples cited above.

18.2 Lessons learned and how to apply them in your own operations.

We will recover the lessons learned from the success stories analyzed in the previous chapter to think about how you can apply them in your own operations based on the SMC. These lessons provided you with valuable information and will therefore be helpful in improving your focus and results as a trader. Here are some key lessons:

Learn from the patterns: Observe the Smart Money behaviors that are repeated in success stories. Pay attention to accumulation and distribution signals, key support and resistance levels, and significant changes in volume. Identifying these patterns will allow you to recognize similar opportunities in the market and make more informed decisions.

Be patient and disciplined: Both attitudes are key for successful traders. They wait for the right conditions before entering a trade and follow their trading plan with discipline, even when faced with adversity. Learn to control your emotions and avoid operating impulsively. Remember that consistency and discipline are key to long-term success.

Combine technical and fundamental analysis– Technical analysis will help you identify key patterns and levels in price charts, while fundamental analysis will provide you with information about economic events and factors that can influence the market. Integrating both approaches into your analysis will give you a more complete and accurate view of the market.

Adjust your approach based on your trading style- Every trader has their own, unique style and personal preferences. As you study success stories, identify the aspects that best align with your trading style and adapt them to your needs. Don't try to copy another trader's strategy exactly, but rather find a way to apply SMC principles according to your approach and personality.

Learn from your own operations: In addition to studying the cases of others, it is essential to learn from your own operations. Analyze your previous trades, both successful and losing ones, and look for patterns and lessons that you can apply in the future. Reflect on your decisions, evaluate your strengths and areas for improvement, and use that information to refine your trading approach.

Applying these lessons to your trading will allow you to: Improve your ability to identify lucrative opportunities, make informed decisions, and manage risk effectively. Remember that trading is a continuous learning process, and each experience, whether your own or that of other traders, gives you the opportunity to grow and improve. Keep an open mind, be adaptable and never stop learning and improving your skills as a trader based on the Smart Money Concept.

19 Challenges and obstacles of Smart Money Trading

19.1 Identification of common challenges that operators face when using SMC

Understanding these types of challenges will prepare you for the moments in which you will have to take measures to overcome them based on a series of criteria or other tools. Below, I present some challenges which are useful to read:

Lack of complete information: Sometimes, traders may not have access to all the information that financial institutions have. This can make it difficult to accurately identify Smart Money accumulation and distribution areas. It is important to use available indicators and tools to obtain as much information as possible and thus make informed and solid decisions.

Misinterpretation of volume and liquidity: the analysis of both levels is fundamental in the SMC. However, incorrectly interpreting these indicators can lead to erroneous decisions. It is essential to have a good understanding of how to interpret volume and liquidity and how to apply them in market analysis. Trading education and experience can help you develop these skills.

Market volatility- The forex market is known for its high volatility; Therefore, sudden and rapid movements can make it difficult to identify Smart Money actions. It is therefore important to adapt to changing market conditions and use flexible strategies that allow you to make decisions in real time.

Risk associated with market manipulation: The SMC involves the recognition and exploitation of market manipulation by financial institutions. However, there is also the risk of being caught in losing trades if the dynamics of manipulation are not properly understood. That's why it's essential to use sound risk management techniques and set clear limits to protect against potential losses.

Influence of external factors: the Smart Money Concept is based on the analysis of the behavior of financial institutions; However, market movements can also be influenced by external factors, such as economic news, geopolitical events, or changes in government policies. Such factors may disrupt Smart Money activity and present additional challenges for traders and their positions.

If you can identify and understand these aforementioned challenges, you will be better prepared when making decisions to overcome them. Remember that successful trading requires continued education, experience and adaptability. As you acquire more knowledge and experience in the Smart Money Concept, you will be better equipped to face these challenges and take decisive measures in your operations.

19.2 How to overcome obstacles and maintain discipline in your trading approach

Obstacles like those noted above can present challenges, but with the right mindset and the right strategies, you can overcome them and improve your results as a trader. Below are some suggestions to overcome these eventualities while always maintaining discipline:

Continuing education- Continue learning about the strategies, indicators and techniques used by Smart Money. Stay up to date with the latest market developments and best practices in trading. Education will give you the confidence and knowledge to deal with obstacles effectively.

Practice patience: Recognizes that the Smart Money Concept does not guarantee instant profits and that success

100

requires time, perseverance and training. Avoid the temptation to operate impulsively and wait for the right conditions to arise before making decisions.

Use a solid strategy: once planned, follow it with discipline. Make sure you have clear entry and exit rules, as well as defined risk management techniques. By having a structured plan, you will be better prepared to face obstacles and avoid emotional decisions.

Evaluate and adjust your approach- Regularly review your trading approach and analyze your past trades. Identify the obstacles you have faced and look for ways to overcome them. If something isn't working, be open to adjusting your strategy or approach. Keep detailed records of your operations and perform retrospective analyzes to identify areas for improvement.

Appropriate risk management- It is essential to maintain discipline in your trading approach. Set clear loss limits and apply risk management techniques, such as using stop-loss and take-profit orders. Make sure you only risk a small, manageable portion of your capital on each trade.

Keep an open and adaptable mind: We have already highlighted that the forex market is constantly changing, so it is important to be flexible and adaptable in your approach. Keep an open mind to new ideas and approaches, and be able to adjust your strategy based on market conditions. Don't hold on to preconceived ideas and be receptive to changes and opportunities that arise.

Overcoming the obstacles of Smart Money Trading and

maintaining discipline in your trading approach takes time, effort and dedication. Still, remember that successful trading is a continuous learning process, and every obstacle is an opportunity to grow and improve as a trader. Furthermore, every eventuality that happens throughout your training will help you test your knowledge and gain more and better experience. With the right mindset and a solid knowledge base, you will be able to overcome obstacles and achieve your goals in Smart Money trading.

20 Use of technology in Smart Money trading

20.1 How technology can improve your ability to track and operate with Smart Money

Technology has revolutionized the trading industry, providing tools and resources that allow traders to access information and analyze the market more efficiently. Below are some ways technology can be used to improve your Smart Money Trading (SMT) approach:

Advanced trading platforms- These offer a wide range of tools and functionalities designed specifically for market analysis. These platforms allow you to follow the movements of Smart Money in real time, access updated charts and price data, and execute your trades quickly and accurately. Using this type of platform gives you a competitive advantage when operating with Smart Money.

Data analysis software: SMT involves analyzing large amounts of data to identify patterns and trends. The use of data analysis software can facilitate this process by allowing in-depth analysis of volume, liquidity and price data. These programs can help you identify areas of accumulation and distribution of Smart Money more efficiently, saving you time and effort.

Alerts and notifications: The technology also allows you to configure personalized alerts and notifications to always keep you informed about Smart Money movements. You can set alerts for certain price levels, specific volumes, or candle patterns, allowing you to react quickly when important events occur. These alerts keep you aware of trading opportunities and allow you to act in a timely manner.

Social networks and online communities: These digital areas have become a very important source of information and analysis for trading. You can join groups and communities of traders where they share ideas and discuss strategies related to the Smart Money Concept. These platforms give you the opportunity to learn from other traders, gain different perspectives and stay up to date with the latest news and trends in the market.

Trading automation: Technology has also enabled the automation of trading, which uses algorithms and automated trading systems to execute trades on your behalf. Although not all traders opt for automation, this option can be useful for those who want to take advantage of Smart Money opportunities quickly and efficiently, without the need to constantly monitor the market.

By taking advantage of the technological tools and resources available, you can improve your ability to track and operate with Smart Money. However, it is important to remember that technology is a complementary tool and does not replace fundamental education, experience and analysis. The combination of an SMC-based approach and the intelligent use of technology can be a powerful strategy in successful trading.

20.2 Recommended tools and platforms for Smart Money analysis.

These tools will help you follow and better understand Smart Money activity in the Forex market. These are some of the most popular options:

Bloomberg Terminal: Bloomberg is a leading financial industry platform providing a wide range of real-time data and analysis. The Bloomberg terminal is widely used by market professionals to access detailed information on volume, liquidity, financial news and more. It provides deep insight into Smart Money movements and is widely regarded as a powerful tool for Smart Money analysis.

MetaTrader 4/5: MetaTrader is a trading platform widely used in the forex industry. It offers a variety of tools and resources for technical analysis, including volume and liquidity tracking. You can use custom indicators and scripts to identify Smart Money patterns on price charts. Additionally, MetaTrader has a large online community where SMC-related strategies and analysis are shared.

TradeStation– Another popular platform used by active and professional traders. It offers a wide range of analysis tools, including volume and liquidity tracking. It also provides the ability to customize your own Smart Money indicators and strategies. TradeStation is known for its robust analysis capabilities and fast order execution.

Thinkorswim: is a trading platform offered by TD Ameritrade. It is known for its powerful set of technical analysis tools and its focus on tracking volume and liquidity. The platform allows detailed analysis of Smart Money movements and offers a variety of custom indicators and drawing tools to identify relevant patterns.

TradingView– Another popular online platform used by traders around the world. Provides interactive charts with a wide range of indicators and technical analysis tools. The platform allows you to perform volume analysis and follow Smart Money activity in real time. Additionally, TradingView has an active online community where ideas and analysis related to Smart Money are shared.

These tools and platforms listed are just a few of the many available for Smart Money analysis. It is important to find the one that best suits your business needs and preferences.

Remember that no tool is infallible and it is essential to complement technological analysis with a deep understanding of the principles of the Smart Money Concept and the Forex market in general.

21   Ethics and regulations in trading

21.1 Discussion on the ethics of Smart Money practices in the market

In this chapter, we will address the issue of ethics in Smart Money practices in the Forex market. While SMC can be an effective trading strategy, it is important to consider the ethical issues related to its implementation. Below are some points to consider in the ethical discussion of Smart Money practices:

Insider information: is one of the most important ethical issues in Smart Money trading. Access to this kind of information, not available to the general public, can allow financial institutions to gain unfair advantages in the market. It is essential to respect the laws and regulations related to the use of inside information and avoid any illegal activity.

Market manipulation- Some financial institutions may engage in trading with the goal of manipulating prices to make profits at the expense of other market participants. These types of practices are illegal and can have negative consequences for the integrity and trust in the market.

Transparency and equity: Smart Money practices must seek to operate in a fair and transparent environment, avoiding actions that could harm other operators or distort the normal functioning of the market. Transparency in transactions and adequate disclosure of information are essential elements in trading ethics.

Responsibility and regulatory compliance: As a Smart Money operator, it is essential to assume responsibility for complying with all applicable regulations and standards. This includes compliance with laws related to trading, disclosure of information and protection of client interests. Maintaining ethical conduct and respecting regulations contributes to the integrity and stability of the market.

Impact awareness- While it is legitimate to look for profitable trading opportunities, it is essential to do so in a way that does not cause unfair harm to other market participants. Ethical responsibility involves considering the impact of our actions and striving to operate fairly and responsibly.

With all that said, we can summarize that Smart Money trading presents ethical challenges that must be addressed responsibly and with respect for laws and regulations. Smart Money traders must seek trading opportunities based on legitimate information and operate in a transparent and fair manner. Integrity and ethics are key elements in maintaining trust and stability in the Forex market.

21.2 Description of existing regulations and how to protect yourself legally.

For this section, it is important to keep in mind that regulations may vary by country and it is essential to consult the applicable local laws and regulations. With this in mind, here are some of the most common regulations and legal protection measures to consider:

Regulations on securities and financial markets- Most countries have specific regulations that supervise and regulate financial markets, including Forex. These regulations can address issues such as transparency, access to inside information, market manipulation, and investor protection. Familiarize yourself with the relevant regulations in your jurisdiction and ensure you comply with them.

Regulatory authorities- There are various regulatory authorities responsible for supervising and regulating financial activities, including Forex trading. These authorities can set standards and norms for market participants, and have the ability to impose sanctions in case of non-compliance. Identify the relevant regulatory authority in your country and stay informed about their requirements and guidelines.

Customer protection- When trading in the Forex market, it is essential to look for regulated financial intermediaries that offer adequate customer protection. Make sure you trade with trusted and regulated brokers, who meet the standards and requirements set by regulatory authorities. This may include fund protection measures, transparency policies and dispute resolution processes.

Contracts and legal agreements- When conducting Smart Money transactions, it is important to have clear contracts and legal agreements that define the terms and conditions of the business relationship. These contracts may include brokerage agreements, client agreements, and confidentiality agreements, among others. Make sure you fully understand the terms and conditions set out in these contracts and, if necessary, seek legal advice to ensure their validity and protection.

Legal education and advice- As a Smart Money trader, it is crucial to be well informed and educated about the laws and regulations that affect your operations. Find reliable educational resources, participate in training programs, and consider seeking legal advice if you have concerns or questions about specific legal issues. Staying up to date and well informed will help you make informed business decisions and protect yourself legally.

Remember that compliance with regulations and respect for laws and standards are essential to operate safely and legally in the Forex market. Legal protection involves: knowing and complying with existing regulations, operating with trusted intermediaries and seeking legal advice when necessary. Maintaining ethical conduct and complying with regulations will contribute to your own protection and the integrity of the broader market. Therefore, stay in line with the various regulations and ethical responsibilities when operating as a trader.

22 The Future of Smart Money Concept

22.1 Perspectives and emerging trends in Smart Money trading.

As the financial market evolves and technologies advance in complexity, new opportunities and challenges arise in the area of SMC. Here are some of the insights and trends that could influence the future of Smart Money trading:

Disruptive technology: Being in continuous transformation, technology in turn alters the way in which trading and market analysis are carried out. Artificial intelligence, machine learning and natural language processing are increasingly being used to analyze large volumes of data and extract relevant information. As technology continues to advance, it is expected that in the future it will provide new tools and approaches for Smart Money trading.

Access to information in real time: With the advancement of technology, traders have access to large amounts of information in real time more easily. This includes volume data, liquidity, buy and sell orders, and other indicators relevant to Smart Money analysis. The ability to obtain information in real time today allows traders to make more informed decisions and take advantage of opportunities in the market.

Big data analysis: Big Data has revolutionized the way financial markets are analyzed. Analysis of large data sets can reveal hidden patterns, correlations and trends, which can help identify Smart Money activity. In the future, big data analysis is expected to continue to evolve, which could provide traders with greater understanding and ability to detect Smart Money operations, as well as think about new types of strategies implementing these types of technologies.

Increased retail participation- With increasing access to financial markets and trading education, the participation of retail traders is expected to increase in the future. This could have an impact on the dynamics of Smart Money, as retail traders could influence certain market movements. It is important to take this trend into account and adapt Smart

111

Money strategies to take into account the growing retail participation.

Regulations and compliance– As Smart Money trading gains popularity, regulations and compliance requirements are likely to strengthen as well. Regulatory authorities could implement additional measures to protect investors and ensure market integrity. Smart Money operators will need to stay up to date on changing regulations and ensure they comply with legal requirements in all their operations.

New financial instruments: As time goes by, new financial instruments may emerge that allow Smart Money operators to diversify their strategies and take advantage of different opportunities in the market. This could include more sophisticated derivative products, blockchain-based smart contracts, or other financial innovations. Being attentive to these new instruments and understanding how they can be used in the context of Smart Money will be crucial to staying up to date in the future.

If we have what is outlined above, we can intuit that Smart Money trading will continue to evolve as technology and market trends advance. Operators will need to adapt to new tools, strategies and regulatory requirements to stay competitive. Staying informed about emerging prospects and trends in Smart Money trading will allow you to take advantage of opportunities and face challenges that may arise in the future.

22.2 How to adapt to changes in the market and new technologies

As the financial environment evolves, it is crucial for Smart Money traders to stay up to date and adjust their strategies to remain effective. Throughout this section, we will present a series of recommendations on how to adapt to these changes:

Stay updated- Follow developments in the financial industry, stay abreast of emerging trends and new technological tools that could be relevant to Smart Money trading. Read specialized books, articles and blogs, attend conferences and seminars, even stay in touch with other traders to share knowledge and experiences.

Learn new skills: With the evolution of the market and technologies, it is important to acquire new skills that allow you to take advantage of opportunities and face challenges in order to get closer to our stated objectives. This may involve learning how to use new data analysis tools, becoming familiar with advanced trading platforms, or gaining knowledge in specific areas, such as blockchain or artificial intelligence. Continuing education and skill development are essential to adapt to changes in the market, as they sharpen its dynamic nature. Learning to use different technologies allows for better readings and interpretations of the large amounts of information regarding the markets on a daily basis.

Experiment with new strategies- As new trends and

113

technologies emerge, Smart Money trading strategies need to be adapted. Don't be afraid to experiment with different approaches and try new strategies to see how they adapt to changing market conditions. Maintain a data-driven approach and carefully evaluate your test results to identify which strategies work best in the current environment. Including such experimentation contributes to knowledge and experience in a comprehensive way to face possible challenges in the future.

Take advantage of technological tools- Use data analysis software, advanced trading platforms and automation tools to optimize your trades. These instruments can: provide real-time information, help you identify patterns and trends, and improve efficiency in the execution of your trades.

Keep an open mind: Adaptability requires having an open mind and always being willing to learn and change to improve. As the market evolves, it's important to be willing to question your assumptions, explore new ideas, and adjust your strategies as necessary. Maintain an attitude of constant learning and be receptive to new perspectives and approaches.

Network of contacts- Maintaining a strong network of contacts in the financial industry can be invaluable in adapting to changes in the market and new technologies. Connect with other traders, industry professionals, technology experts and participate in online communities related to Smart Money trading. These connections can provide you with up-to-date information, opportunities for collaboration, and a supportive environment where you can share ideas and experiences.

We must remember that adapting to changes takes time and effort. Keep an open mind, be patient, and be committed to continuing to learn and improve. With an adaptive approach, you will be in a strong position to face the challenges and take advantage of the opportunities that the market and new technologies present.

23 The order blocks

Order blocks are a trading tool that refers to a price zone on a chart where there has been a large concentration of limit orders waiting to be executed.These areas represent a significant level of demand or supply in the market.Order blocks are identified on a chart by looking at previous price action and looking for areas where the price experienced significant movement or sudden changes in direction.. Traders using this method look for areas where heavy buying or selling activity has occurred in the past, which could act as areas of support or resistance in the future.

23.1 Types of order blocks

The types of order blocks will depend on both the area in

which they are located and the reaction caused to the price. Often, order blocks are the last candle before a bullish or bearish movement is generated.

Bullish order blocks: This is the last bearish candle before a bullish movement takes place. It is called bullish (a metaphor related to the upward attack of the bull) because you have to wait for the price to rise again to be able to buy.

Bearish order blocks: in this case we are talking about the last bullish candle that is prior to a bearish movement. It is called bearish (derived from the metaphor of the bear's downward attack) because it is necessary to wait for the price to fall to have the opportunity to sell.

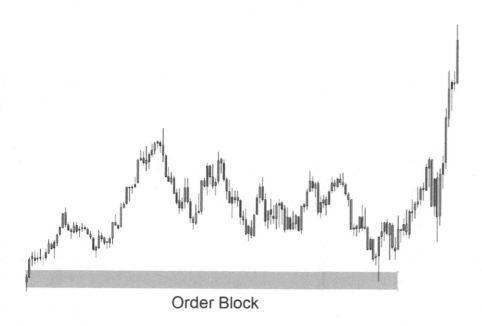

Order Block

We can see in the graph that the price returns to the area to collect pending orders and in the end the trend continues to rise.

Order Block

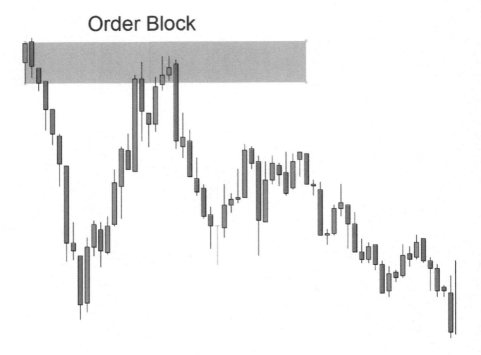

We see in the chart that the price returns to the zone to collect pending orders and in the end the trend continues to decline.

23.2 Breaker block

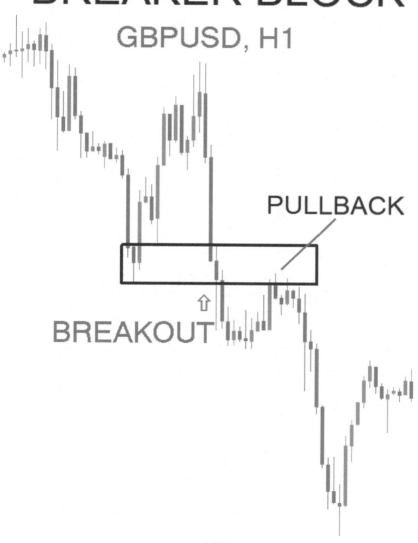

BREAKER BLOCK

GBPUSD, H1

PULLBACK

BREAKOUT

It is true, there may be cases in which an Order Block is not fulfilled and the price goes through it very strongly, as can be seen in the graph. In these cases, one way to trade is to go down to the 5 minute or even 1 minute chart and wait for a Pullback.

Pullback Trading consists of waiting for the price to make a small retreat towards the Order Block that has been crossed with force. When the price approaches this level again, we take the opportunity to enter a sell trade, based on the continuation of the bearish direction.

This strategy is based on the idea that the price often tends to retrace towards significant levels after a sharp movement. By taking advantage of this pullback, we can enter the dominant direction of the market and take profits when the price continues in that direction.

By moving down to shorter time frames, such as the 5-minute or 1-minute chart, we can more accurately capture these pullback movements and enter the trade more quickly. This allows us to reduce risk and maximize profit potential.

As you can see in the chart above, this strategy can result in successful trades that develop quickly into the positive. It is an effective way to operate when an Order Block is hit hard and does not fulfill as expected.

23.3 Order Block Primary Impulse

ORDER BLOCK Primary Impulse

As we can see in the previous chart, when the first impulse candle is smaller than the previous candle and of a different color, we will take the first impulse candle as a reference to plot the Order Block in favor of the trend.

This approach is based on the analysis of the candlesticks on the chart. When the first impulse candle is smaller than the previous candle and of a different color, it indicates a possible decrease in the Momentum of the trend. However, if the direction of this candle is consistent with the prevailing trend, we still consider this momentum as part of the overall trend.

Therefore, to plot the Order Block in this scenario, we take the first impulse candle as a reference, since it represents the beginning of the movement in the direction of the trend.

This approach allows us to more accurately capture the beginning of the bearish or bullish movement, ensuring that our Order Block is aligned with the prevailing market trend.

By using the first momentum candle as a reference to plot the Order Block, we can more effectively identify accumulation or distribution zones where large market participants are likely to make important decisions.

Of course, in case the trend is bearish, the principle remains the same, but in reverse. That is, when the first impulse candle is smaller than the previous candle and of a different color, we will take the first impulse candle as a reference to plot the Order Block in a bearish direction.

This approach is based on the analysis of the candlesticks on the chart. When the first impulse candle is smaller than the previous candle and of a different color, it indicates a possible decrease in the Momentum of the downtrend. However, if the direction of this candle is consistent with the prevailing trend, we still consider this momentum as part of the overall trend.

Therefore, to plot the Order Block in this bearish scenario, we take the first impulse candle as a reference, since it represents the beginning of the movement in the bearish direction. This approach allows us to more accurately capture the beginning of the bearish movement, ensuring that our Order Block is aligned with the prevailing market trend.

By using the first momentum candle as a reference to plot the Order Block, we can more effectively identify accumulation or distribution zones where large market participants are likely to make important decisions. This gives us a better understanding of market dynamics and helps us make more informed decisions when trading in the financial market.

23.4 Micro Range Order Block

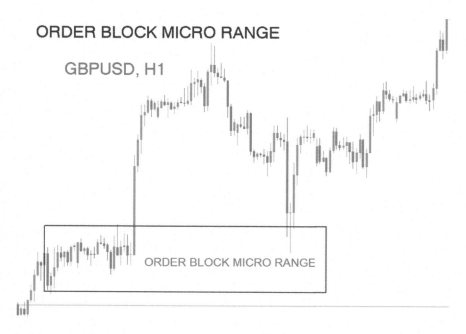

Micro ranges are quite common in the market and refer to a condition where the price compresses, often preceding a sharp breakout. When the price compresses, that is, when it moves in a tight range, this can indicate a build-up of pressure that will eventually be released in a specific direction.

During this period of compression, micro ranges can form, which are small areas on the chart where the price moves sideways in a narrow range. These micro ranges can be seen as blocks of orders that are gradually filling throughout the range.

When price finally breaks out of this micro range strongly, it is said to have created an order block. This means that the price has accumulated a significant number of buy or sell orders during the compression period, and once the range is broken, these orders are activated, generating a quick and strong move in the direction of the breakout.

To explain it with an example, in the previous chart we are in an upward trend. During this trend, the price begins to compress into a narrow range, forming a micro range. During this time, traders are accumulating both buy and sell positions, thus creating an order block.

When the price finally breaks higher out of this micro range, the accumulated buy orders are activated, causing a pronounced bullish move. This bullish movement is reinforced by the accumulation of orders in the order block, which generates additional upward momentum.

In short, micro ranges are areas of compression on the chart that precede a sharp breakout. When price breaks out of a micro range strongly, it is said to have created an order block, which indicates an accumulation of orders and can result in a significant move in the direction of the breakout.

23.5 Validate an Order Block

ORDER BLOCK VALIDATE

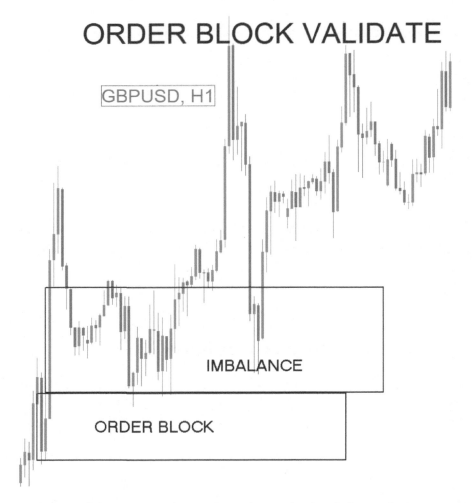

GBPUSD, H1

IMBALANCE

ORDER BLOCK

A powerful order block is when it is followed by an Imbalance. An Imbalance occurs when there is a clear discrepancy between supply and demand in the market. In other words, in a bullish order block, a positive imbalance means that demand far exceeds supply, suggesting a high probability of a significant bullish move. Similarly, in a bearish order block, a negative imbalance indicates that supply exceeds demand, suggesting a pronounced bearish move.

Furthermore, it is crucial that this order block has not been mitigated. This means that there has been no price action that has invalidated the original order block. For example, if a bullish order block is followed by a large bearish candle that completely encompasses the order block, this would indicate that the order block has been mitigated and would no longer be considered powerful.

Therefore, when identifying a strong order block, we look not only for the accumulation of significant orders, but also for a clear imbalance in supply and demand, followed by confirmation that the order block has not been mitigated by price action. . This provides us with a solid and powerful signal to make trading decisions with greater confidence.

24 The imbalances

Imbalance is an imbalance between buy and sell orders. This is a concept widely used in trading; Imbalances or price imbalances are a positive phenomenon since they open up opportunities in the trader's operations.

We can see it in the charts, they are long candles where after a while they are usually tested again; Since, by quickly passing through that area, large participants are left with many unperformed operations, therefore, having to pass through the same place to be able to execute pending orders.

This Imbalance pattern is a clear sign of market imbalance. To identify such a pattern, simply take sequences of three candles and look for wide-range candles that barely overlap the upper and lower wicks of adjacent ones. That is, there is a price range within that large candle that does not touch the range of the previous or subsequent candle, leaving a kind of gap.

The size of this gap is obtained by measuring the distance between the maximum of the previous candle and the minimum of the subsequent one (bullish case), or the minimum of the previous candle and the maximum of the subsequent candle (bearish case).

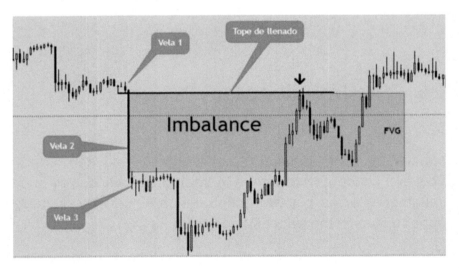

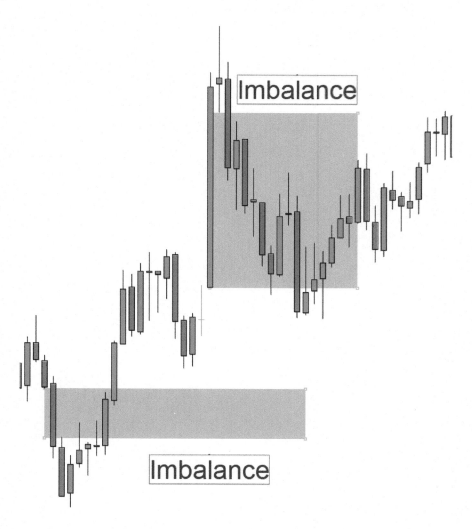

Imbalances are drawn with a rectangle that takes the free

part of the candle, observing the previous and subsequent ones.

24.1 Operate imbalances

24.1.1 Trading in favor of price

In this first scenario, we operate using the Imbalance in favor of the trend. We observe that the trend is downward. In this case, we wait for the price to return to the Imbalance, and once it enters the Imbalance again, we switch to a shorter time frame. For example, since we are in the 1 hour (H1) time frame, we go down to 5 minutes or even 1 minute. In this new shorter time frame, we observe precisely when the price begins to change direction. At that moment, we open the operation by placing the stop-loss above the imbalance, and we adjust the take-profit according to the price movement. We can choose to partially close the operation as the price advances, and lower the stop loss, or let it run until the end, but taking into account that this strategy, when it goes well, is usually very profitable. The risk-reward ratio can be as high as 1 to 10, showing that this trade can be highly lucrative.

24.1.2 Waiting for the price to move away from the Imbalance

In this specific case, when the imbalance forms, we mark it on the chart and wait for the price to move away from this point. Next, we look at a chart of a lower time frame, such as five minutes or one minute. At this time, we close a sell trade when we see a return pattern observing the price direction change. Afterwards, we wait for the price to return to imbalance to pick up the pending trades that were left there as a result of the imbalance between supply and demand, as explained above, and at this point we close the trade. Getting a good result. At each Maximum we can make a purchase with a good distance from the stop loss and in the end when it reaches the imbalance we close them all.

24.2 When to use order block or Imbalance (FVG)

To determine whether it is more appropriate to use order blocks or imbalances (FVG) when trading Forex or other markets, it is essential to take into account the general context of the market and the specific scenario in which you find yourself. Each tool has its own strengths and is best suited to certain market conditions.

Firstly, order blocks are particularly useful when you are trading within an established trend. These blocks represent areas on the chart where Smart Money has accumulated large volumes of buy or sell orders. In an uptrend, for example, bullish order blocks can serve as entry or exit points, as they indicate areas where the price is likely to react and continue its upward movement. Likewise, in a downtrend, bearish order blocks can point out areas where the price could bounce or retrace.

On the other hand, imbalances (FVG) are more effective when you are looking to capture sharp movements or breakouts in the market. An imbalance occurs when there is a significant discrepancy between supply and demand at a specific price level. These imbalances can indicate strong buying or selling pressure in the market, which can result in rapid and sharp movements in price. Therefore, imbalances are particularly useful for identifying key levels where significant price action is expected, such as resistance or support breakout points.

Ultimately, combining both tools can offer a more complete view of the market and help you make more informed trading decisions. For example, you could use order blocks to identify entry and exit points within an established trend, while imbalances could serve as additional confirmation or to identify more aggressive trading opportunities on breakouts of key levels.

In summary, when selecting between order blocks and imbalances (FVG) to trade, it is crucial to adapt your approach to the market context and your specific trading objectives. Both tools are valuable and can complement each other to improve your analysis and your ability to capitalize on market opportunities.

25 Traps or manipulations of strong hands in Forex

The foreign exchange market or Forex is one of the largest and most liquid financial markets in the world, as we have explained in previous chapters. However, it is also a market where "strong hands" such as financial institutions, central banks and large investors participate, which can influence price movements. Here are some "traps" that retail traders should watch out for when facing strong hands in Forex:

Price manipulation- Strong hands can influence prices through massive buy or sell orders. This can cause retail traders to enter positions at the wrong time, following the direction that strong hands want them to go.

Stop-hunting- Strong hands can also see the stop-loss levels of retail traders and thus move the market to activate those orders, which usually results in losses for the retailers.

Sudden volatility- Even these large players are capable of creating sudden volatility in the market through unexpected announcements or policy changes, which can cause retail traders to lose money if they are not prepared.

Disinformation: We have mentioned on several occasions the access to privileged information, through which they can spread false or misleading information and thus manipulate the market to their benefit.

As a curious fact, generally the hoaxes tend to occur during London and New York times. Within Asian time there is usually little movement, so strong hands are usually not interested.

To protect yourself from these traps, we can take into account a series of suggestions:

Use stops discreetly and place stop-loss and take-profit orders at logical levels, not just where everyone else has them.

- Perform your own fundamental and technical analysis instead of relying solely on external sources or trading signals.

135

- Diversify your portfolio to reduce the risk of a single position that can be affected by strong hands.

- Maintain proper risk management and do not get carried away by emotion.

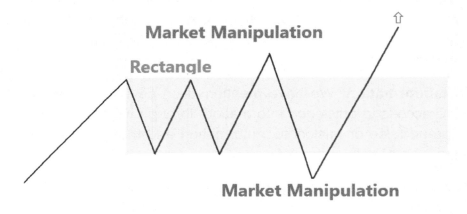

In this chart we can see a flag or rectangle where the strong hands carry out two manipulations to collect liquidity to ultimately make the real breakout.

On this chart we see something similar to the previous one, although here on a real EUR/USD chart.

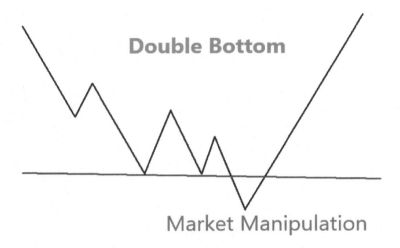

Double Bottom

Market Manipulation

The following chart presents a double bottom with manipulation, in which they collect liquidity by breaking the stop losses and then making the actual break. This action could be compared to the double top.

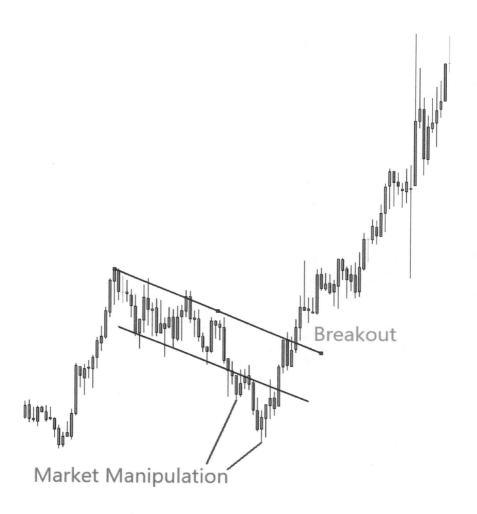

Market Manipulation

Breakout

Here we can observe a double manipulation in a flag; In the end, the real breakage is generated, always collecting liquidity.

Market Manipulation

Other examples of manipulation. When these "traps" are present, the graphs usually do not turn out to be harmonious. Logically, the big players make these movements in order to collect liquidity from retailers. The directions and changes that occur throughout the graph are carried out at the whim and discretion of these "strong hands".

Market manipulation

Market manipulation

Market Manipulation

Manipulations like those set out above usually occur in the patterns of rectangles, flags, channels, double tops or triangles. In all the graphs, a similar behavior is observed, to a greater or lesser extent: a false breakage prior to the real breakage. This clearly influences the behavior of retail investors and generates profits for large shareholders.

The ZigZag indicator can be useful when wanting to detect possible movements of these strong hands. The appearance of this type of indicator can give us the hypothesis of the operations that may be happening and opens up possibilities for how we could act accordingly.

Another indicator that can be useful to detect this type of manipulations is the RSI divergences.

RSI divergence

The point here, both in the previous graph where another example of manipulation is displayed and in the previous ones, is the need to practice and in this way be able to recognize these events in real time. If we achieve this, we will be more difficult to deceive and we will even have the knowledge and experience to follow up on strong hands without being kicked out of the market.

147

26 Practical strategies

26.1 The liquidity

Liquidity plays a crucial role in trading strategies, especially for those who follow the Smart Money concept. In the world of investments, liquidity refers to the ease with which an asset can be bought or sold in the market without significantly affecting its price. But what does liquidity really imply when we look at the charts?

Liquidity can come in a variety of forms, and understanding it is essential for traders who want to make informed decisions:

Featured Highs and Lows: High and low points on a chart represent liquidity levels. These are the points where buyers and sellers are most active, creating areas of strong interest and trading volume.

Double Top or Double Bottom Patterns: These patterns are indicative of areas where liquidity has been particularly high. A double top represents a level where the price has tried to rise twice without success, indicating strong resistance and possible bearish reversal. On the other hand, a double bottom is a level where the price has tried to fall twice without success, suggesting solid support and a possible bullish reversal.

Bearish or Bullish Trend Lines: Bearish and bullish trend

lines represent the general direction of price in the market. When an uptrend line is drawn, it connects rising price lows, while a bearish trend line connects falling highs. The interaction of price with these lines can provide signals about the strength or weakness of liquidity in the market.

Liquidity is a crucial factor for institutional investors as they need to execute large orders without causing drastic price movements. These investors look for areas of high liquidity to enter or exit positions without problems. However, sometimes even with sound analysis and correct market direction, positions can lead to losses due to lack of liquidity at the time of execution.

Therefore, understanding how to identify and take advantage of liquidity on charts is essential for any trader looking to maximize their chances of success in the financial markets.

Liquidity is money whose existence in the market indicates the presence of big players. Therefore, price always follows liquidity. Part of the liquidity is the levels where most traders' STOP LOSS orders are recorded. These ranges are usually behind important supports and resistances, historical tops and bottoms, psychological levels, trend lines, etc. This is why we recommend checking these levels carefully before entering the trade because the market will probably move towards these levels to collect liquidity in the market. future.

26.2 Trends

Understanding trends is crucial for any trader looking to track Smart Money and maximize their opportunities in the market. However, this understanding goes beyond simply looking at a graph in a single unit of time. Institutional investors, who often lead market trends, conduct analysis across multiple time frames to identify and capitalize on opportunities over a longer time horizon. Therefore, it makes sense for traders to follow this approach and trade in the same direction as these big players.

Market trends can be seen on different time scales, from minutes to months or even years. By studying trends on larger time frames, traders can better grasp the overall direction of the market and avoid getting caught up in short-term swings.

However, it is important to be careful when following trends, as mistakes can occur and financial losses can be sudden. Even when trading in the same direction as Smart Money, there are inherent risks in the market that can lead to losses. For example, a false signal may lead to premature entry into a position, or the market may experience a sudden change in trend direction.

Therefore, it is essential that traders implement proper risk management and be prepared to adapt to changing market conditions. This includes setting stop loss levels to limit losses, diversifying trades to reduce exposure to a single asset or market, and staying informed about economic and geopolitical events that can influence market trends.

In summary, following market trends over multiple time frames can be an effective strategy for online trading with

Smart Money. However, it is crucial to be aware of the risks and maintain sound risk management to protect yourself from significant financial losses.

To study the Smart Money trend you can use the DOW THEORY.

The Dow Theory It is a fundamental pillar in technical analysis and a key concept to understand how financial markets move. Developed by Charles H. Dow, one of the founders of the famous Dow Jones & Company and co-creator of the Dow Jones Industrial Average (DJIA), this theory is based on a series of principles that describe the general behavior of the market.

One of the main tenets of the Dow Theory is the idea that market prices reflect all relevant news and events. In other words, prices move according to the collective perception of market participants about the economy, politics and other factors affecting financial assets. This premise suggests that changes in market prices are driven by changes in underlying fundamental conditions.

Additionally, the Dow Theory states that markets move in trends. These trends can be bullish, bearish or sideways, and can occur on different time frames. Dow identified three phases in any trend: the accumulation (or distribution) phase, the trend phase itself, and the distribution (or accumulation) phase. During the accumulation phase, smart investors (or "Smart Money") are accumulating positions in anticipation of a future trend. During the trend phase, prices move in the predominant direction, either up or down. Finally, in the distribution phase, Smart Money begins to

151

liquidate its positions, leading to a change in the trend.

Furthermore, the Dow Theory emphasizes the importance of trading volumes. Dow believed that volumes should confirm price movements. For example, in an uptrend, volumes are expected to increase as prices rise, indicating strong market interest. Likewise, in a downtrend, volumes should increase as prices fall.

Dow Theory provides a solid framework for understanding how financial markets move and for identifying trading opportunities. By paying attention to trends, confirmation, volumes, and other key principles, traders can make more informed decisions and improve their ability to anticipate market movements.

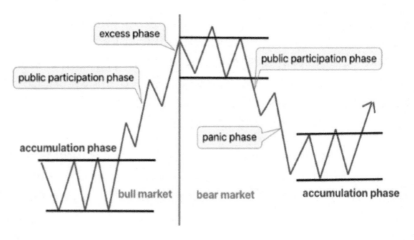

This theory allows understanding the trend of the SMC, if used in higher time units, to intervene in lower time units, in line with the underlying trend. Once the trend is identified, the only thing left to do is understand how Smart Money traders operate in the markets!

The concepts related to Smart Money aim to enable the trader to discover the "footprints" left by large institutional traders, commonly known as the "strong hands" or "smart money" through the graphs that account for their transactions, whether purchases or sales, of large magnitude. The fundamental premise is to identify the price trend and the precise moment in which the institutional operator executes the operation. Taking advantage of these traces or clues of significant price movements allows the trader to operate extremely precisely, often obtaining trades with a high risk/reward ratio.

To achieve this precision, the Smart Money operator is dedicated to identifying major price trends on long-term charts and then descending to shorter time-scale charts and executing operations from there with the desired precision. Typically, trading is carried out on a chart that is approximately fifteen times smaller than the main one where the trend has been identified. In this strategy, we will focus on trading on one-minute charts with detecting trends and points of interest on fifteen-minute charts. However, it is important to note that this strategy can be successfully applied in other time frames depending on the trader's preferences and strategies.

26.3 In an uptrend

By carefully observing the chart, we identify a clear bullish trend, supported by the tracing of a trend line that confirms the succession of increasing highs and lows. This ascending pattern signals positive momentum in the market. Then, to confirm the strength of the trend, we will plot a BOS (which we will develop below) on the breakout of the existing structure.

By marking this break, we establish an order block at the break point of the structure. This, located at the breakout low, represents a key level that can indicate a change in market dynamics. It is worth noting that all of these observations are made in a fifteen minute time frame on the EUR/USD pair.

The next step is to analyze the same pattern on a shorter time frame, specifically one-minute charts. The purpose of this is to verify if there is any entry opportunity in the previously identified order block. This strategic approach, which uses multiple time frames, provides a more complete view of the market situation and allows for more informed decisions by considering both the general trend and the specific details of the order block in a shorter period of time.

26.4 Breakdown of structure (BOS)

The Breakout of Structure (BOS) is a crucial signal in the market which indicates that the price is about to change direction. For example, when the price reaches a new low and a lower high, it means that the market structure has been broken, which is the first indication that the market is preparing to reverse downwards.

In this scenario, it is advisable for every trader to adjust their strategies to trade in the direction of the upper BOS time frame. This implies that when the price closes above or below a high or low, serious consideration should be given to adjusting trades to align with this signal.

The graph clearly illustrates the breaks in the structure.

Every time the price breaks above the previous high, a breakout of the structure is identified. A change in character (ChoCH) is then observed as the price falls below the previously established lows. This change indicates a possible reversal in market direction and can be a crucial time to adjust trading strategies accordingly.

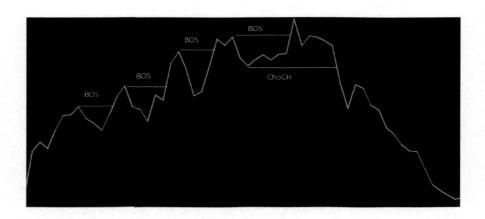

Continuing with the observation on the fifteen-minute chart of the EUR/USD pair, we confirm the bullish trend that we have previously identified. We thus clearly mark the order block, mentioned above, and notice that it coincides with the BOS, which is established as the future stop in case we obtain an entry in the order block.

The next step is to move to the one-minute time frame to

157

evaluate if an opportunity to enter the previously identified order block presents itself. This approach, which involves analysis over multiple time frames, provides us with a more detailed perspective on the market situation. By considering both the general trend and the specific elements of the order block and its relationship to the bos, we are better equipped to make informed decisions and capture potential trading opportunities.

26.5 Change in trend (CHOCH)

ChoCh in trading means a fundamental change in the trend orThe term "CHOCH" "Chain of Character" or "Chain of Character." This expression is used to describe a sudden change in price direction in financial markets. The CHOCH indicates a sharp change in market dynamics, breaking with the previous trend and suggesting a possible change in direction.

When a CHOCH occurs, the price stops following the established trend and shows the opposite behavior. For example, if the price was rising, the CHOCH would indicate a sudden reversal to the downside, and vice versa.

This term is mainly used in the field of intraday trading, where traders seek to take advantage of these rapid changes in price to make profits. Identifying a CHOCH can be an important signal to open a new position or close an existing position, depending on the trading strategy of each trader.

In summary, CHOCH in trading is a sudden change in price direction that breaks the previous trend, which can represent a trading opportunity or a risk for traders, depending on how they manage it.

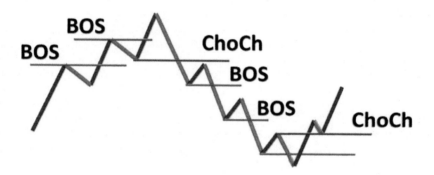

CHOCH

In the previous chart there is a downward trend and the moment the last maximum is exceeded, with a candle that has closed above, it creates a trend change and this specifically is a CHOCH.

26.6 Point of interest

The term "POI" in trading refers to "Point of Interest". In the context of trading, a POI is a level or area on the chart that traders consider significant due to its relevance to the price.

POIs can be identified in various ways and may include:

Support and Resistance Levels: These are areas where the price has had difficulty breaking through in the past (resistance) or where it has found support in the past (support).

Fibonacci Levels: Based on Fibonacci retracement levels, these levels are areas of possible trend reversal or continuation.

Pivot Points: These are mathematically calculated levels that can serve as significant areas of support and resistance.

Relevant Highs and Lows: These are the highest and lowest points in a specific time period that may be important to traders.

Congestion Zones: These are areas where the price has been oscillating in a narrow range for an extended period, indicating indecision in the market.

They can also be an Order Block, an Imbalances, or the sum of the two, taking the entire area.

POIs are important to traders because they represent areas where the price is likely to react. Many traders use these points to make market entry or exit decisions, set their stop-loss and take-profit levels, or simply to get an idea of the likely price direction.

In short, POIs in trading are levels or areas on the chart that traders consider significant due to their historical or technical importance, and can influence trading decisions.

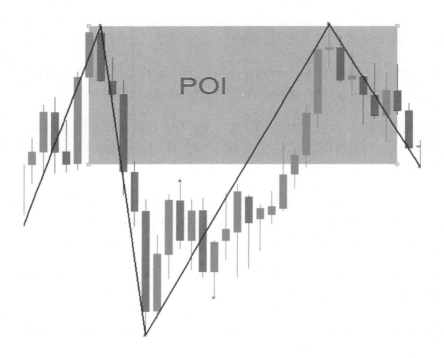

26.7 Example of executing an Order Block

Smart Money Concept 3.0 PRO

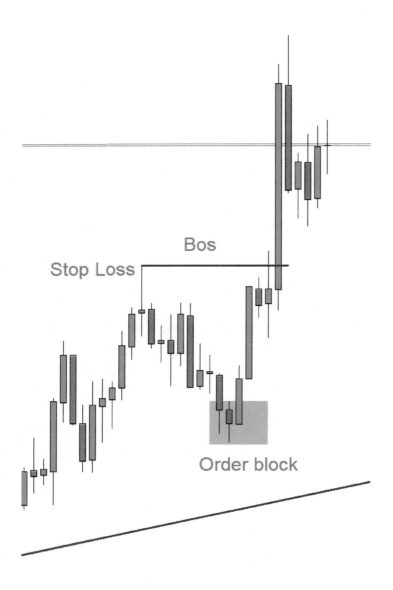

Smart Money Concept 3.0 PRO

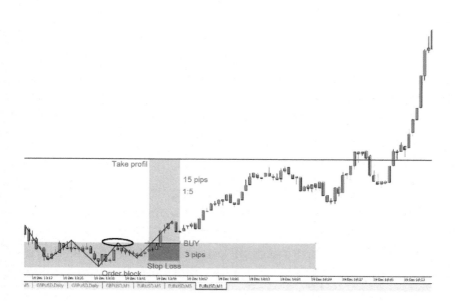

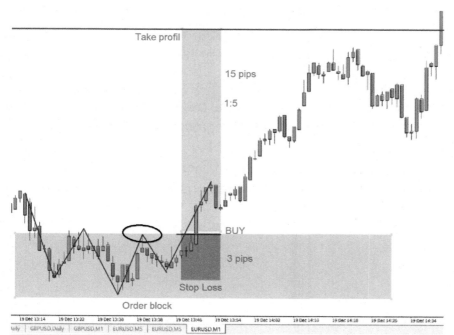

We expect the price to return to the order block we marked earlier on the 15-minute chart.

And we move on to the one-minute chart of the EUR/USD pair, where we have previously marked the order block, we observe a structure break at a maximum that we have identified and indicated with an ellipse. From this break, by overcoming said break, we identify the opportunity to make an entry into the market.

To execute this entry, we place the stop-loss below the last low, which in this case is equivalent to approximately three pips. Additionally, we set a take-profit of fifteen pips, thus creating a risk/reward ratio of one to five. It is therefore crucial to highlight that we have opted for a conservative take-profit, since we could have established one to ten, as evidenced in the fifteen-minute chart. In a more aggressive scenario, this would have been achieved, generating a profit of between thirty and forty pips easily.

On the one-minute chart, we present two visualizations: one general and one zoomed in to allow a more detailed look at the trade. This strategy, which combines the identification of structure breaks and the use of favorable risk/reward ratios, demonstrates the versatility of analysis in different time frames for making informed decisions in intraday trading.

26.8 Distribution zone break

We can clearly see a distribution phase on the fifteen minute charts. After an upward trend, an area is evident where the market has consolidated its gains, marking a change in the structure of the trend. This transition materializes by breaking the distribution zone, generating a minimum and establishing a new direction now downwards. This change in dynamics is crucial as it indicates a transition from an uptrend to a sideways phase and finally to a downtrend.

In this context, we can execute a block order in the fifteen-minute interval, and simultaneously plot the take profit level. Then, to fine-tune the entry and validate the trade, we move to one-minute charts. In this shorter time frame, we evaluate whether a concrete opportunity arises to enter the previously established block order.

This strategic approach, which combines analysis at different times, allows us to more accurately capture key moments in the market and make informed decisions. Detailed observation of the distribution phase on fifteen-minute charts and subsequent validation on one-minute charts are part of a comprehensive strategy to optimize the execution of operations in the financial market.

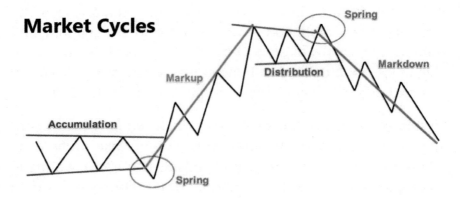

Smart Money Concept 3.0 PRO

EUR/USD 15 M

Distribution

Order block

TAKE PROFIL

| 14 Dec 09:15 | 14 Dec 13:15 | 14 Dec 17:15 | 14 Dec 21:15 | 15 Dec 01:15 | 15 Dec 05:15 | 15 Dec 09:15 | 15 Dec 13:15 | 15 Dec 17:15 | 15 C |

| GBPUSD,M5 | GBPUSD,Daily | GBPUSD,Daily | GBPUSD,M1 | EURUSD,M5 | EURUSD,M5 | EURUSD,M15 |

EUR/USD One Minute Chart

We observe in the range of one minute that it effectively gives us entry.

On the one-minute chart of the EUR/USD pair we identify the order block previously marked on the fifteen-minute time frame. We clearly observe a downward trend that culminates in a minimum represented by an ellipse. Then, entry is made once this minimum is surpassed, which marks the breakout point.

When executing the entry in such a scenario, we set a stop-loss of eight pips and a take-profit that exceeds forty pips. This thus generates a risk/reward ratio of one to five. Such a relationship is especially attractive for trading on one-minute charts; Since, given the dynamic nature of this time frame, several trades can be made in a single day due to how quickly the market moves.

This strategy focused on identifying trends and taking advantage of entry opportunities on one-minute charts demonstrates the agility and versatility required to trade effectively in an intraday environment. The combination of accurate analysis and favorable risk/reward ratios contributes to the potential profitability of trades carried out in this time frame.

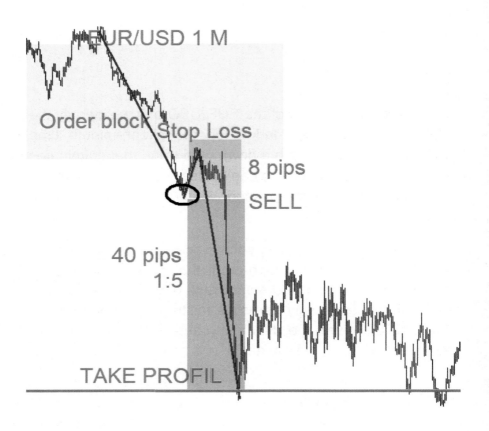

M5 | EURUSD,M1

What we have just analyzed by relating fifteen-minute charts to one-minute charts offers a quick and dynamic perspective of the market. However, it is worth noting that this strategy could also be effectively implemented with a thirty-minute chart alongside a one-minute chart. In that case, the risk/reward ratio would double, meaning that while we could make half as many trades in a work day, each trade would have a greater potential profit. In general, the trader must choose two terms: one higher and one lower, where there is at least a difference of seven periods and each one adapts to their way of operating.

Each trader must adapt this strategy to their trading style and preferences. Furthermore, it is essential to observe trends over longer time frames to always trade in favor of the prevailing trend. Although this may mean waiting longer to make moves, trading in the direction of the long-term trend is usually a recommended practice.

An additional strategy could be to closely follow the eight major currency pairs, observing their movements and setting alarms for them. That is, when an alarm is triggered, we will perform a more detailed analysis within the shortest period to confirm a possible entry. Trading in this way, that is, always in favor of the trend of longer time frames, can generate successful trades with a positive ratio of between 80% and 90%, as long as they are carried out with precision and discipline.

26.9 Bearish order block

In this example, we find a bearish Order Block on the GBP/USD chart, specifically on the one-hour time frame. We identify the Order Block as the last rising candle before the decline. Next, we move to the 5-minute chart to watch the price return to the Order Block. After a detailed analysis, we place the sell order at the final line of the Order Block, placing the stop loss slightly above the last maximum, at a distance of 16 pips from the sell order. Additionally, we set the take profit at 105 pips, resulting in a ratio of almost 1:7. As can be seen, the operation is satisfactory.

This example illustrates the concept of "smart money", where professional traders use technical analysis and pattern observation to make informed decisions in the market. By identifying the Order Block and strategically placing sell orders, stop loss and take profit levels, you maximize profit potential and reduce risk.

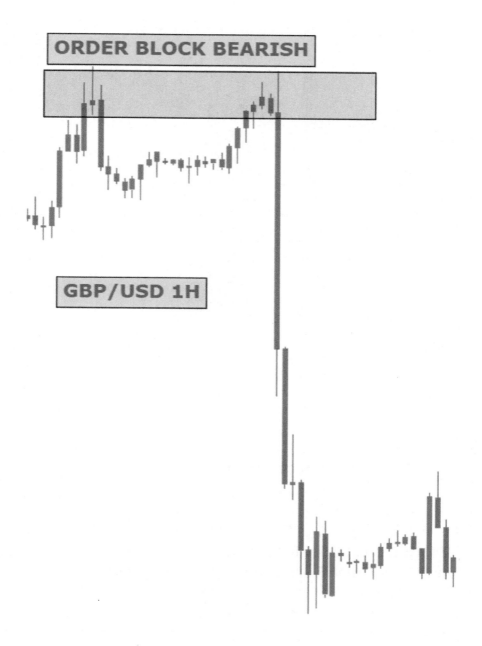

Now we move on to the 5-minute GBP/USD chart.

26.10 Bullish order block

In this example, we find a bullish Order Block on the GBP/USD chart, specifically on the one-hour time frame. We identify the Order Block as the last down candle before the rise. Next, we move to the 5-minute chart to watch the price return to the Order Block. After a detailed analysis, we placed the sell order on the top line of the Order Block, placing the stop loss slightly below the last minimum, at a distance of 9.40 pips from the buy order. Additionally, we set the take profit at 93.10 pips, resulting in a ratio of almost 1:10. As can be seen, the operation is satisfactory.

This example illustrates the concept of "smart money", where professional traders use technical analysis and pattern observation to make informed decisions in the market. By identifying the Order Block and strategically placing sell orders, stop loss and take profit levels, you maximize profit potential and reduce risk.

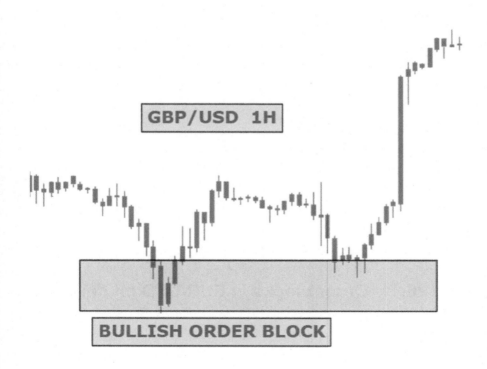

GBP/USD 1H

BULLISH ORDER BLOCK

Now we move on to the 5-minute GBP/USD chart.

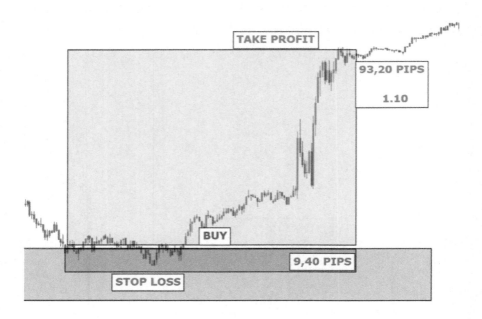

26.11 Order blocks in EUR/USD on daily chart

On the EUR/USD chart, in the daily candle frame, we focus on looking for Order Blocks within a downtrend. We will enlarge the image so that you can clearly see the trend and the different Order Blocks that we have identified.

First of all, we look at the bearish trend on the EUR/USD daily chart. We identify the points where the price has formed decreasing highs and lows, confirming the bearish direction.

Then, we look for the Order Blocks within this trend. An Order Block is characterized by being an area where supply exceeds demand, which precedes a bearish movement. These blocks usually represent areas of accumulation or distribution by large market operators.

Zooming in, we can see several Order Blocks along the downtrend. Each of these blocks represents an area where sell orders have accumulated, indicating the possible continuation of the downtrend.

By identifying these Order Blocks, traders can use them as reference points for selling trades, placing their sell orders at strategic levels within these blocks. Additionally, stop loss and take profit levels can be placed in a way that maximizes profits and minimizes losses in case of adverse movements.

This strategy of identifying and trading around Order Blocks within a downtrend is an example of the concept of "smart money", where professional traders use technical analysis to make informed and profitable decisions in the forex market.

Here we enlarge the image a little, so you can see them better.

Now we draw the Bos, which mark the structure breaks and the impasses, which are areas where the strong hands have left unexecuted sales orders.

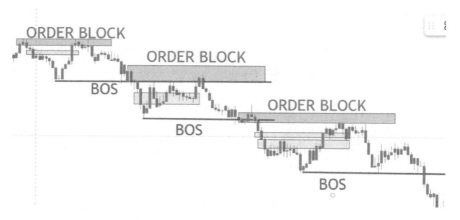

On the EUR/USD chart, in daily candles, we are going to analyze the Order Blocks and imbalances separately to be able to appreciate them better. The constant presence of imbalances indicates that the price is more likely to return to the Order Block.

First, we focus on Order Blocks. These are areas on the

181

chart where buy or sell orders have accumulated, creating an imbalance between supply and demand. In the context of a downtrend, Order Blocks often precede significant bearish movements.

Looking at the chart, we identify several Order Blocks throughout the downtrend. Each of these blocks represents an area where significant resistance or a buildup of sell orders has formed. These zones can be important reference points for selling trades, as they indicate areas where the price is likely to retreat.

On the other hand, imbalances are imbalances between supply and demand at a certain price level. These imbalances may indicate areas where a large order volume has built up, suggesting a high probability of the price returning to that level in the future. In the context of a downtrend, imbalances are signals that the price is likely to retrace towards the Order Block.

By studying imbalances separately, we can identify specific areas where supply or demand has outpaced the counterpart, giving us clues about possible trend reversal or continuation levels.

By combining the observation of Order Blocks and imbalances, traders can make more informed decisions about their trades, taking advantage of supply and demand signals to maximize profit potential and minimize risk. This is fundamental in the "smart money" strategy, where we seek to operate intelligently by taking advantage of market movements.

ORDER BLOCK

IMBALANCE

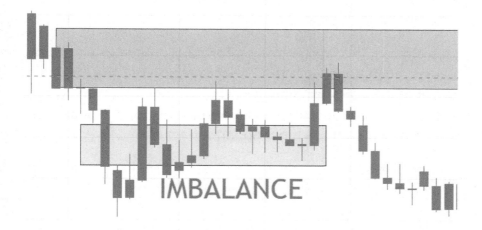

ORDER BLOCK

IMBALANCE

Once we have observed on the daily chart that the price returns to the Order Block, we descend, for example, to the one-hour chart to better refine the entry. We wait for the price to leave the Order Block in a bearish direction and execute our entry, applying the stop loss above the last maximum and the take profit with a minimum ratio of 1 to 10.

This strategy allows us to look for very profitable trades by taking advantage of the confirmation of the bearish movement in shorter time frames. By moving down to the one-hour chart, we can fine-tune our entry and ensure that we are entering at the most opportune time.

Placing the stop loss above the last high helps us limit our losses in case the price moves against our trade, while setting the take profit with a risk-reward ratio of at least 1 to 10 allows us seek significant profits in relation to the risk

184

assumed.

By applying this strategy, traders can maximize profit potential and reduce risk, allowing them to effectively capitalize on market opportunities in the direction of the prevailing trend. This is a common practice within the "smart money" approach, where we seek to operate intelligently and profitably in the foreign exchange market.

27 Last conclusions

27.1 Key SMC Concepts

In this last chapter, we will summarize key concepts of the Smart Money Concept, which we have covered throughout the entire book. Below are its main points:

Smart Money: refers to large financial institutions and institutional operators that have a significant impact on the market. These entities possess a large amount of capital and resources, allowing them to influence price movements.

Understanding large institutions: understand how large financial institutions operate in the market; since their participation can have a considerable impact on the direction of prices and trends.

Volume and liquidity analysis: both are essential to follow the Smart Money activity. Changes in volume and liquidity can provide clues about the involvement of financial institutions and institutional traders.

Accumulation and distribution patterns: Smart Money tends to accumulate or distribute positions in certain areas of the market. Identifying these zones and patterns can help you detect trading opportunities.

Price patterns and candles– By learning to interpret these patterns, traders can gain a deeper understanding of market movements.

Specific indicators- These indicators can provide useful signals for making trading decisions.

Order blocks and imbalances: are the blocks of orders that remain pending in certain areas and the market imbalances manifested in long candles, respectively.

Risk management: Proper management is essential when operating with Smart Money. It is essential to set loss limits and use risk management strategies to protect against significant losses.

Adaptability and discipline: Operators must adapt to changes in the market and new technologies. Keeping an open mind, acquiring new skills, and using technological tools can help you stay current and competitive.

In conclusion, the Smart Money Concept is a way to understand and take advantage of the activity of large financial institutions in the market. By understanding how these institutions work and using specific tools and strategies, traders can make more informed decisions and improve their trading results, generating profits and getting closer to the goals and objectives set out in their respective plans.

Final recommendations:

Continue learning: Trading is a constantly evolving field, so it is important to continue learning and stay constantly updated. Stay up to date with the latest trends, tools and strategies in Smart Money trading.

Practice with discipline: Trading requires discipline and constant practice. Spend time regularly testing your strategies and improving your analysis skills.

Manage your risk: Never underestimate the importance of proper risk management. Set loss limits and use risk management strategies to protect your capital.

Keep regular records- Keep a detailed record of your operations and results. This will allow you to review your performance, identify areas for improvement, and make more informed decisions in the future.

Be patient and realistic- SMC trading requires patience and realism. Don't expect instant profits, and remember that there will be periods of losses. Keep a long-term perspective and be realistic with your expectations.

With these recommendations in mind, you will be on your way to making the most of the Smart Money Concept and improving your trading in the financial market. Good luck on your journey as a Smart Money operator!

27.2 Practical tips to apply the SMC in your trading

Finally, here are some practical tips to apply the Smart Money Concept in your trading:

Practice patience and discipline: Don't get carried away by emotions and avoid making impulsive decisions. Wait for the right conditions to arise before entering a trade and set clear loss limits and profit targets.

Use a risk management strategy- Set an appropriate position size in relation to your capital and set loss limits. Use stop-loss orders to protect against excessive losses and consider the risk-reward ratio with each trade.

Keep a trading journal- Record all your trades in a trading journal. Write down the details of each operation, including the input, the output, the reason for the operation, and the results. This will help you evaluate your performance, identify patterns and recurring errors, and make necessary adjustments to your strategy.

Develop a trading plan- Similar to financial planning in the early chapters, build a solid trading plan based on the SMC.

Define your objectives, strategies and entry and exit rules. Stay firm with your plan and avoid getting sidetracked by emotions or fleeting speculation. Your plan is what should last throughout the time you have organized.

Maintain a long-term focus: Don't be discouraged by occasional losses and keep a long-term perspective; Successful trading happens over the long term. Keep learning, improving your skills, and adjusting your strategy based on changing market conditions.

28 Summary

It's time to say goodbye. In these pages of Smart Money Concept we have thoroughly explored the fascinating world of this sophisticated approach, unraveling strategies that will take your trading to higher levels. From detailed volume and liquidity analysis to skillful interpretation of price patterns and strategic use of specific indicators, we have traveled a path full of guides and key concepts used by large financial institutions and institutional investors.

During reading this book, you have acquired skills to: identify areas of accumulation and distribution of Smart Money, recognize patterns in price charts and take advantage of areas of high trading probability. Additionally, you have discovered how to use candlestick patterns, indicators, and technical analysis to make informed decisions and improve your trading.

But we have not limited ourselves to just reviewing strategies; We've also delved into the essential mindset of trading like Smart Money by reviewing: the importance of discipline, proper risk management, and solid trade planning. We share success stories, lessons learned and the importance of adapting to changes in the market and emerging technologies.

We cannot ignore ethics and regulations, which ensure that your operations are fair under legal parameters. Additionally, we have examined the crucial role of technology in Smart Money trading, including recommending various tools and platforms to boost your analysis and monitoring of the markets.

Finally, this book has attempted to provide practical recommendations and advice to apply in your trading. We have encouraged you to adapt to the challenges of the market and maintain a solid mindset to make the most of the opportunities that Smart Money offers.

In summary, Smart Money Concept Advanced Strategies has equipped you with a complete set of tools and knowledge to operate with confidence in the financial markets. We hope that this book inspires you and has provided the necessary foundation to achieve success in your trading career. Apply these advanced strategies from the Smart Money Concept and make your operations more profitable and effective!

If you have enjoyed reading this book and found value throughout its pages, I would love for you to share your experience by leaving a review on Amazon. Your opinion is crucial and can help other readers discover the benefits and insights this book offers.

If you consider that this book has been useful, informative and has contributed to improving your trading skills, I invite you to rate it with five stars. Your support and positive comments are a great motivation for me and help me to continue sharing valuable knowledge.

I thank you in advance for your time and support. I hope you continue to have success in your trading and that the Smart Money Concept strategies continue to give you great results! Thank you so much!

About the author:

Over the years, Luis has invested tirelessly in his trading education and professional development. He has completed numerous specialized courses and read countless books on the subject. His thirst for knowledge and disciplined approach have led him to become a highly successful trader. Luis has studied Economic Sciences at the Complutense University of Madrid.

However, Luis' journey to success was not easy. Like many other traders, he has faced challenges and obstacles along the way. However, his perseverance and determination led him to overcome difficulties and become a consistent and profitable trader.

Throughout his career, Luis has accumulated valuable experience in a wide variety of trading strategies and risk management. He has developed a solid and disciplined approach, based on a deep understanding of the markets and the ability to make rational decisions in high-pressure situations.

Luis has also shared his knowledge and experience with other traders, acting as a mentor and coach for those who wish to improve their skills and achieve trading success. His hands-on, results-oriented teaching style has been instrumental in helping many enthusiasts develop a winning mindset and achieve their financial goals.

Briefly, Luis Risueño Gómez is a prominent trader and educator in the field of trading. His extensive experience, solid knowledge and disciplined approach make him a benchmark within the industry. Thanks to his dedication to continuous learning and his passion for trading, he has managed to live a life of success and financial freedom.

Luis Risueño Gómez

Printed in Great Britain
by Amazon

45122641R00116